What People Are Saying About Darren Starwynn

"This book is engaging from the start due to your writing style, which includes personal stories shared, open-hearted encouragement to the reader and humorous comments sprinkled throughout. The book is a love letter to life with a blueprint for living it as consciously as one can. You impart so much practical and philosophical wisdom in the book that it will retain value as a reference book that many will want to return to for continued support over the years. I think it's a gem for anyone involved in the pursuit of self-knowledge and their connection to humanity and Spirit."

Debra Bentley
Acupuncturist

"I am very happy to have met Darren. He led me to another spiritual space and healing energy spectrum, huge and limitless. I just opened a new window in my healing field and I am very excited about newer, broader and deeper (spiritual, physical, emotional energy fields) journey in my future life. Thank you very much!"

Ming-Sung Ahn
Acupuncturist

"I felt a tremendous release of trauma that has been embedded in my tissues for decades."

Melanie H
Artist, musician

"Dr. Starwynn, you are very connected and extremely eloquent in presenting an as yet unknown field and reality. I have enjoyed the blending of physics, quantum and Spirit."

Aurora Konig
MS, AP, Dipl. Ac

D1446783

"Imagine my immeasurable good fortune to have you appear in my life, to find you, just the right person who can guide and navigate me in and through my request to wake up. I can't remember feeling this much relaxation and ease in my body. And no more headaches!"

Sharon N
Client

"A lot of the negativity and depression started fading away, and changes in my personal and professional life started to happen."

Raoul. G
Tech developer

"I have finally found someone who helped me by working with root causes, to feel better physically, mentally and spiritually."

Helen B
Psychotherapist

"I am a mortgage broker and mother of 3 children. I recently had two healing sessions with Darren Starwynn. This was a new experience for me and it was amazing! I experienced feelings of deep connection to my spiritual source, and waves of energy moving through my body. It was super relaxing and it felt like all kinds of deep discomforts and anxiety melted out of my body. I came with some nagging back pain and it was gone after the first session. I have been a regular meditator for years, and I do healing work myself, but this felt like a whole new level of connection that I loved.

Tisha S
Client

"Please, please keep doing what you are doing. No one is doing this spiritual work for healers. Not the way you do. I am increasing my vibrational quickly and exponentially."

Kristine Buckley
Acupuncturist

Also by Darren Starwynn O.M.D.

Healing the Root of Pain

Microcurrent Electro-Acupuncture

DARREN STARWYNN, O.M.D

RECLAIMING YOUR CALM CENTER

TRANSFORM INNER PAIN
TO INNER PEACE BY TURNING DOWN
THE NOISE IN YOUR MIND

foreword by
BEVERLY RUBIK, PH.D., BIOPHYSICIST.

Photography by:
Jane Richey Photography

Cover by:
Elias

Library of Congress Control Number: 2017911061

ISBN-13: 978-0578195360

This book is dedicated to the true Self within us all,

the experience of which sets us free.

Acknowledgements

This book would not be possible without the education, support, inspiration and blessings I have received from so many people. I wish to express my gratitude to all of the souls who have generously shared their knowledge with me that I have been able to prove out in my personal experience and integrate into this book. Since it would not be possible to name them all, here are some.

My father Abe shared many wise and silly things with me, and one of my favorite was his teaching about "mini-gurus". He said that while there are many of the famous "big" gurus around who are publically known and have lots of followers, there are many more mini-gurus. Those are ordinary people who inadvertently deliver bits of perfectly timed wisdom to us when we really need it. Another way of saying this is that Life is my teacher. So I acknowledge the long procession of mini-gurus who have blessed my life each day when I was paying attention.

I also wish to acknowledge my mother Temme who taught me so much about living life fully and gave me so much support and encouragement on my path. I am also grateful to my sister Laura who encouraged me in writing this book and kindly helped me edit the cover text. I also acknowledge my daughter Sonya for teaching me the deepest lessons about loving and Jane Richey who has taught me much about my heart and masterfully took most of the pictures in this book. Also Andoni Panici and Deanne Wilson who served as the models for most of the photographs. I am grateful to those who reviewed my manuscript and offered their valuable feedback: Alan Plenty, Bruce Roberts, Dana Horvath, Debi Weiss, Debra Bentley, Kevin Barr, Peri Ozkar. Beverly Rubik and Jane Richey.

I honor all the spiritual teachers who have mentored, inspired, uplifted, awakened or frustrated me at different stages of my life. These include Prem Rawat, Devra West, Zhi Gang Sha, Maria Sunukjian and others not listed, plus many more who are in the spirit world.

I honor my mentors of medicine and healing: Susannah Redelfs, Deborah Wayne, Charles McWilliams, Meg Benedicte, Jon Whale, James Pinkman, Bill Berlin, Steve Miller, Reinhold Voll, Yoshio Manaka, Peter Mandell, Dinshah Ghadiali, Robert Becker and many more.

I am very grateful to Jo Ann Rathgaber, whose tireless support and hard work helped me produce over 40 live seminars. Her generosity of spirit and big heart touched our clients and made my life so much easier. Also to Teri Sherman and Debi Weiss whose smart and elegant teaching inspired and informed hundreds of our students.

I also acknowledge Shima Moore who originally gave me the original push to write this book, and Peter Fairfield who welcomed me to Marin County, California back when I did not know anyone else here.

Finally I am grateful to Beverly Rubik who is a foremost researcher into the human biofield and kindly agreed to write the foreword for this book.

How to Use This Book

There are two ways you can use this book:

1. By reading it from beginning to end like most books. It is set up in a logical progression in which each section builds on the previous ones.

2. As a reference book you can use as an ongoing guide for developing your practice of meditation and self-realization.

The book is divided into four sections, as follows. I have included many cross-references throughout the book to make it as easy as possible to get needed information relating to the part you are reading.

Section I: Weapons of Mass Distraction

This section includes perspectives, facts and references to help you understand why our minds often seem so overactive or disturbed nowadays. You are likely to read some perspectives that are new to you here. Some of this may inspire you, enlighten you, disturb you or piss you off. If any of those happen this section is serving its purpose in presenting new ways to understand the conundrum we find ourselves in on Planet Earth now.

I suggest that you read this section first before doing the practices in Section II. If you are eager to start your meditation practice right away go for it. Just read through Section I as you are experiencing the practices in Section II to deepen your understanding of their value.

Section II: How to Heal Yourself and Reclaim Your Calm Center

Here you will find techniques and guided meditations for reclaiming your calm center and increasing your joy of life. These methods take advantage of the neuroplasticity of your brain to literally rewire you back to inner balance and vitality.

Chapter 8 - Practice Plan contains an 8 week, step-by-step plan for gradually developing or updating your daily meditation practice. These practices are valuable whether you are just starting to meditate or have been doing it for decades.

To make it as easy as possible to start implementing the meditation practices I have put resources on my website to support you in the form of video guided meditations and meditation practice instruction sheets. See Appendix 2 in Section IV for instructions for accessing these.

Section III: New Healing Methods

This section offers information that will be valuable if you need professional support on your healing journey. It contains a chapter about new methods of vibrational medicine and a chapter about Biofield Healing. These are methods that can significantly accelerate your healing process when you need support or simply want to accelerate your spiritual development.

Section IV: Where to Go From Here

This section offers guidance and practical resources for your self-healing process and living a conscious, fulfilling life. It also contains a Resource section.

Writing Challenges and Conventions

Terminology: In Appendix 1 in Section IV you will find a glossary of unusual or metaphysical/spiritual terms used in this book. These are words that may be unfamiliar to many readers, or could be interpreted in multiple ways. If these terms are new to you please keep this section bookmarked so you can easily refer to it as you read the book.

Each time a new term from another language or tradition is introduced I have *italicized* it. These terms are not italicized after their first introduction.

Language Gender: In line with many other authors I have arbitrarily alternated between the terms "he" and "him" and "she" and "her" when making general statements. This is preferable to constantly using the terms "them" and "their". My use of the male or female gender in these statements is not intended to imply that either sex is more likely to have the experiences referred to.

In a similar way I have given some real or hypothetical examples through some stories, in some cases using a woman as an example and in some cases a man. Again, these choices were not intended to imply that either men or women are more susceptible to the issues being described.

Spiritual/Metaphysical Beliefs: In some of the chapters, particularly *Chapter 5; The Dark Side of Your Mind,* I have included references to some often controversial beliefs such as the existence of past lifetimes, cross-cultural pain bodies and shifts of consciousness happening on Earth now. It is not necessary that you believe in these ideas in order to gain benefit from the practices presented in Part II. Those will work for you regardless of your belief systems.

These metaphysical concepts are presented to open your mind to considering new possibilities of where inner pain and blockage may have originated. Consider those explanations and embrace them if they inspire you and if not, let them go.

I personally don't believe that my beliefs are all that important. I have seen how they have changed throughout my life. What is most important to me is what I actually experience for myself. Please use this book in that spirit – consider the ideas and try out the practices presented, and then discover what resonates within you.

Foreword

$\mathbf{D}$o you feel overwhelmed, discontented, disconnected from your deepest self, and yearn for something more? Do you suffer from depression, fear, worry, anxiety, obsessive-compulsive behavior, or insomnia? Do you have disease? Are you having serious relationship issues? Are you concerned about the state of the world, or what you can do to help? Are you unclear about the purpose of your life? Are you interested in being a healer, or if you already are one, moving further on your path? If your answer is "yes" to any of these questions, then this book is for you.

For so many of us, our lives feel like an endless treadmill of menial tasks sidelining our life purpose. We are overwrought with do-ing and not spending enough time be-ing. Our whole world has sped up, thanks to the increasing clock speed of technology that delivers an information deluge on a daily basis for us to muddle through. We are more connected than ever by technology, yet more disconnected from ourselves and each other than ever before.

We struggle and trudge along throughout life. On top of all this, we have ongoing threats of terrorism, global climate change, pandemics and political uncertainty across the globe, alongside escalating wars, mass immigration, lethal doses of radioactivity spreading out from Fukushima, and other world dramas to deal with. New stressors confront us, from the "chemtrails" sprayed across our skies to the wireless radiation from our communication devices, making us "guinea pigs" in global experiments.

Our food is genetically modified, processed, and tasteless, so it's no wonder we are more overweight than ever before. Mainstream media, with its "shock and awe," breeds fear, anger, and addiction to bad news. We are chronically ill or worry about getting chronic disease. Needless to say, we are more drugged than ever, with Big Pharma's campaign to sooth every symptom with drugs, making us numb and inert. Indeed, our stress level has reached a new norm—like the perpetual "code orange" alert at our airports.

It is no wonder that more and more of us suffer symptoms from distress, post-traumatic stress disorder (PTSD), and related conditions. This book points out that most of us are probably suffering from "low-grade" PTSD. "We cannot thrive personally or collectively at this heightened level of distress.

Many self-help books have been written in an attempt to help the human condition, but most of them are just blabber, because they just try to talk us into new ways of being. Einstein once said that it is impossible to solve a problem at the same level of consciousness that created it. A new approach is necessary if humanity is to survive, one that will allow us to move to new heights and thrive.

This book is different because it helps us cultivate our higher dimensional self, our calm center in the eye of the hurricane, through a wide variety of practical exercises. When we are at our calm center, it changes the way we perceive things, and the things we perceive can change, too. After all, we are spiritual beings having a life experience in a lower dimensional world in order to grow and evolve. This book helps us access our higher dimensional consciousness by mobilizing our intention and attention. This is our gateway to awakening and self-healing.

The Chinese character for "crisis" is said to mean "danger" plus "opportunity." We are experiencing extraordinary dilemmas at this critical transition time in order to help us personally and collectively transform to a new level of being. The book offers a psychospiritual view of our spiritual transformation and evolution as a natural process, which I find encouraging and comforting. In chaos theory, increasing disorder always precedes large scale change to a new level of order and being. So transformation is inherently a messy ordeal, and we are approaching the crucial turning point along the way.

The reader can examine him/herself via a checklist of karma, curses, vows, and unfinished business of past lives that may be complicating his/her present life. Then, in the greater part of the book, the author offers numerous practical exercises aimed to access higher dimensional consciousness for spiritual evolution and self-healing, drawing on Buddhist, ancient Greek, and Jungian teachings; energy psychology; breathwork; energy medicine; and many mind-body modalities. In addition, there are instructive videos on the author's website that complement the book to guide and assist the reader in these exercises. Along the way, the author reveals many personal stories of his own transformative journey, including some from his patients, which are real gems.

I am delighted to find a whole chapter dedicated to biofield healing. The biofield or human energy field is regarded as the organizing field of life that regulates the physiology and biochemistry and maintains life's integral wholeness. The biofield exists in the physical realm and also in higher dimensions as our subtle bodies—the astral, energy body, and mental body. Back in the 1990s at the National Institutes of Health (NIH) I led a task force that developed the biofield terminology and concept, deemed necessary to explain how certain types of alternative and complementary medicine, especially energy therapies, work. Clinical evidence shows that biofield therapy (energy healing) that delivers and redistributes bioenergy is very effective with pain and mood disorders, among other conditions. It also increases overall well-being.

Because of its accessibility and conversational style this book is a valuable complement to scholarly works on the biofield and quantum energy. It is a guidebook and practice manual that is concise and user-friendly. In short, this is a book for our challenging times that has the potential to change your encounter with life.

Beverly Rubik, Ph.D.

President and Founder, Institute for Frontier Science
Professor, Energy Medicine University
Adjunct Faculty, College of Integrative Medicine and Health
Sciences, Saybrook University
Oakland, California

www.frontiersciences.org
www.brubik.com

CONTENTS
∞

1

Introduction

It is easier to tame the wild north wind
than it is to control the human mind[1]
-- KRISHNA

Do you know who you really are?

Here is what I know. You are a conscious being with unlimited creative potential. You are made of the stuff of love, and it can be no other way. You are sovereign. This means that you are the creator of your own experience, and no one else truly has power over you. Any areas of your life in which others seem to be calling the shots are those areas in which you have agreed, on some level, to give your sovereign power away.

And we have done this big time. We have agreed to be less than we really are in so many ways. We have given our power away to parents, family members, teachers, clergy, partners, lawyers, politicians, gurus, bankers and world leaders. Many of us have given our power away in other unseen and unspoken ways. As we gave our power away we started to experience some combination

---

[1] Quote is attributed to the God-man Krishna from the Indian scripture *Bhagavad Gita*

of fear, pain and isolation. In order to try to protect ourselves from our fear and ease our pain we have made additional agreements with those we have believed could help, save or love us. This has made our web of agreements even more complex and convoluted.

This complex web of agreements is the stuff that makes up the *"monkey mind"* that so many people talk about. This is the experience of our thoughts rapidly flitting from one thing to another, like monkeys jumping around tree branches. Having our minds in this condition greatly cuts down on our inner peace and enjoyment of life. The pain caused by our overactive minds has led us into all manner of diversions, compulsive behaviors and addictions in order to get a few moments of respite from the inner noise. It has made the pharmaceutical industry the most profitable business in the world. And it is what makes so many people say *"I just can't meditate, my mind is too active and it just doesn't work for me."*

We are much more powerful than we know. You have probably heard this famous quote from author Marianne Williamson:

> *"Our deepest fear is not that we are inadequate. Our deepest fear is that we are powerful beyond measure. It is our light, not our darkness that most frightens us. We ask ourselves, who am I to be brilliant, gorgeous, talented, and fabulous? Actually, who are you not to be? You are a child of God."*
>
> **-- MARIANNE WILLIAMSON**

"Our deepest fear is not that we are inadequate. Our deepest fear is that we are powerful beyond measure. It is our light, not our darkness that most frightens us. We ask ourselves, who am I to be brilliant, gorgeous, talented, and fabulous? Actually, who are you not to be? You are a child of God."

Put aside all the other things you've heard, read or believed about meditation and the process of healing yourself from pain and fear. Put aside, even for a little bit, any dashed hopes and disappointments that arose because it seemed like nothing really changed after all the healing work, therapy and spiritual practices you have done. Put aside any belief that you are not enough or that there is something wrong with you.

This book will take you on a journey into greater self-knowledge that can fundamentally change the way you see yourself and your world. It provides new answers and practical solutions to the following vital questions:

- *Why are my issues and struggles still in my face after so many years of diligently working on myself?*
- *What are the hidden reasons that growing numbers of people are suffering with chronic anxiety, post-traumatic stress disorder (PTSD), panic attacks, OCD (obsessive-compulsive disorder) and more?*
- *How can we free ourselves from these experiences and live confidently and joyfully from a place of inner calm?*
- *For people who believe "I just can't meditate" what are some simple and effective ways to go within and enjoy inner peace?*

REVISITING YOUR INNER PEACE

People have been talking about inner peace for a long time. Almost all spiritual paths, religions, self-help books and healing workshops claim to bring people on a path to peace of mind. Here's a funny thing though – hardly any of the people I have known who have pursued all these paths and workshops (or taught them) feel that they have truly gained lasting inner peace.

If you ask them about it, and they trust you enough to tell you the truth, more likely they will tell you how negative and stressful thoughts are still bothering them and stressing them out much of the time. There seems to remain a very persistent part of our minds that "has a mind of its own", and is far from peaceful!

There is a new word that very well describes the tone of experience in our society these days. The word is *discombobulation*.

This word is now found in English dictionaries, and a commonly accepted definition is:

A stunned or bewildered condition

I would expand on this definition of discombobulation to include the following experiences, which are becoming increasingly common.

- Feeling overwhelmed
- Overactive mind that keeps you feeling off balance
- Loss of clear purpose and direction in life
- Fluctuating between clarity, and inspiration (higher consciousness) and anxiety or depression (lower consciousness) without any reason
- Feeling like time is speeding up - you race all day to get things done then collapse in exhaustion at the end of the day
- Having new inspiring visions for your life but feeling frustrated because you can't seem to realize them
- Strange pains and health problems, come and go, and no one really understands them

You will learn about some of the hidden causes of discombobulation in *Chapters 4* and *5*.

Here is a quote from Megan, a 33 year old marketing rep in San Francisco. Her story is typical of people who are experiencing discombobulation:

"I've been trying to live a healthy lifestyle and be a conscious human being for years. I've read zillions of self-help books, done podcasts from gurus and experts, taken yoga and meditation classes and more. But I still feel stressed out much of the time and don't feel good about where I am in my emotional life. None of my relationships with guys have turned into what I really want and my stress levels are actually increasing. I was self-medicating with booze

and pot but have gotten away from that since my body just can't handle it any more. Why is it so hard to feel good about my life?"

I have heard hundreds of stories like this from my clients, and at times have dealt with my own version of it. There is no shortage of psychological and spiritual explanations for this modern human dilemma.

If you are one of those people who have searched through many healing methods, paths and practices you will find some familiar ideas here. But these will be just part of a bigger picture that may, literally, blow your mind and take you into a whole new world of self-empowerment and self-realization.

WHAT IS YOUR CALM CENTER, AND WHY YOU NEED TO RECLAIM IT

The term *"calm center"* refers to the inner part of you that has always been peaceful and joyful. It has been there throughout all your ups and downs. Your calm center is already fully connected to all the love, freedom, abundance, energy and opportunity that you could ever wish for. This part of you has never been wounded. It requires no improvement, no enlightenment and no healing – it is already perfect and complete. Best of all, it is not "pie in the sky", not "woo-woo", not theoretical and you don't have to have any special abilities or psychic powers to enjoy it.

All you need to do is to care enough about your freedom and fulfillment to reclaim it.

So why should you care? Why is it important to reclaim your inner calm center?

I like to make things very practical. Here are just a few of the benefits you get by reclaiming your calm center:

> •Your self-confidence increases because you deeply **experience** that you are never alone

- It is hard for people to "push your buttons" or "yank your chains" because you already have what you most need, and so people can't easily manipulate you

- You are connected with unending love 24/7 even while you are going through all the natural ups and downs of your life. So it is much easier to fulfill the old saying "Don't sweat the small stuff. P.S. – it's all small stuff".

- You will learn to become more unshakeable in the face of stress. Even if you do feel scared or upset sometimes this part of you will be like a solid rock that will carry you through

- Clarity will come to you about your most fulfilling life path

- In general, you will feel less blocked or stuck in old, negative ways of thinking and relating with others, and freer to boldly move forward creating the life of your dreams

Your calm center is what keeps you grounded and secure within yourself. It is the perfumed garden within your soul where you always know yourself to be OK, no matter what dramas of life are swirling around you. Your calm center is your fountain of self-love, the part that can say "no" when necessary to people and situations that are not good for you.

The calm center has been known by many names. Some have called it *Tao*. Some have called it essence. Some have called it higher self. Some have called it the Divine Self, or God within. Some have simply called it the *Self* (with a capital S). *Self* is the term that will be used most frequently in the rest of this book.

LIVING IN THE EYE OF THE HURRICANE

I'm sure you know about those hurricanes that sometimes ravage the southeast USA. Even though destructive winds could be howling at 70 - 150 miles per hour on the outer part of the hurricane there is always a calm, peaceful area in the middle called the *eye*. Birds can fly in a leisurely way in the eye, and airplanes have even been able to fly safely there. Crazy, huh?

Our minds also have a calm center that is just like the eye of the hurricane. Our calm center is always available to us, even when we feel emotionally triggered.[2] This is a really good thing because it is very hard, and sometimes impossible, to control the hurricane winds of our minds.

The key here is not in struggling to control our minds. I and millions of others have tried that until we are blue in the face without accomplishing it long-term.

The key is to get friendly with your calm center and learn how to be there whenever you want. Now these two things, controlling the mind and being in your calm center can sound like the same thing but they are not. One is an effort to change, which takes

2 You will be able to experience this for yourself by working with the practices in Section II

enormous energy, and the other is simply relaxing and being with a part of you that already is.

Grab a small object and hold it in your hand. Then open your hand and let it fall. How hard was that? That is how easy it can be to let go of inner struggle and be in your calm center. You will learn powerful, yet simple practices to help you be there in Section II.

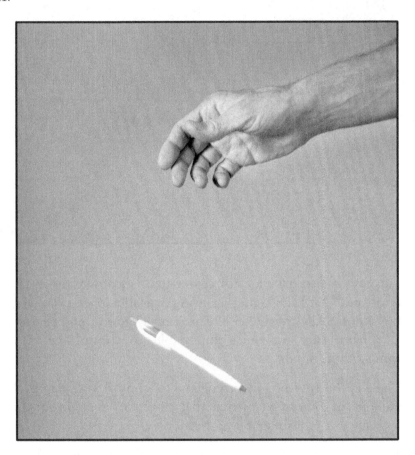

You may have heard a lot of this before in various spiritual books and teachings. What is different here is that by doing the practices you will have a direct experience of the Self, not just read one more concept about it. Your calm center is something that is totally possible for you to experience just the way you are right now. There is nobody too damaged to experience their calm center. That is a false and cruel belief. I know you can do it because you are alive and breathing. As you start on this journey get ready to purge old beliefs that have created pain and separation in your life.

Each religious leader or spiritual teacher brings their own belief system or cultural background to what they teach. Most of these teachings have value, yet many of them are more complicated than is really necessary. Many of them are also tied into unnecessary belief systems not based in the sovereignty of the practitioner. What is most needed on Earth now are practices that are ultimately simple. If you follow any true path it can take you back to the Self. But it may take a long time. What you will learn here can work for you quickly if you give it a chance.

Being in touch with your calm center does NOT mean that your outer life will remain calm and uneventful! You will still experience a lot of exciting and disruptive things, and many ups and downs. It DOES mean that you can enjoy a measure of inner peace through it all. And even see it all as fun - and laugh more.

WHY I AM WRITING THIS BOOK

This book reflects my own life experiences as well as countless hours of study and research. While I have decades of clinical experience working with clients the message of this book is also very personal. I have been through extensive trauma myself, and have struggled with my own experience of PTSD (post-traumatic stress syndrome) since early childhood. There will be more about *PTSD* in *Chapter 2,* and you will gain new insights that are probably very different than what you have already heard about it.

Most people who have suffered with PTSD know why they have it. They are either a military veteran who has been through the horrors of active duty in a war zone, have been through other traumatic experiences as adults or they grew up in a violent or abusive home where they felt terrified, helpless or ashamed. Some people have experienced all of the above.

In my case the causes for my PTSD were not so obvious. My parents were basically supportive and kind to me. After I graduated from high school in 1970 and faced the military draft for the war in Vietnam I got a high lottery number and didn't have to go. My family was far from wealthy, but we never wanted for our basic needs.

In spite of all these blessings I grew up feeling emotionally shut down and full of fear. I was smashed on the head and sent to the hospital when I was 4 years old, and then had another concussion at age 10 after being struck on the head again by a moving car. When I got older and was in junior high and high school I was often bullied, and sometimes the guys who bullied me were smaller than me. I felt lonely and alienated and was drawn to use of marijuana and LSD during some of my teenage years.

Even though my youth was often painful I was always aware of an innate sense of wholeness and goodness. It felt like there was this part of my consciousness that was always there whispering to me that life was really amazing, and that if I just hung in there everything good would eventually come to me. As a result of this inner connection I never got majorly depressed or suicidal because that part of me knew everything was OK.

By age 19 I was living in Boulder, Colorado and was burned out on the use of drugs. That year I was drawn to study with a spiritual master called Maharaji who had come to Boulder from India. I am grateful to that teacher because he showed me a simple meditation method that helped me go within and start experiencing my calm center. I traveled to India with Maharaji that year, and started on a long commitment to spiritual practice and self-healing that has never ended.

After I returned from that trip I spent most of my 20's meditating daily and doing service projects throughout the USA. Since then I have had the privilege of studying with several other high level healers who guided me in how to deeply heal myself and help heal others.

My path as a doctor and healer started in earnest when I was 30 years old and began my training in acupuncture and Chinese Medicine in south Florida. Since then I have had healing practices in Connecticut, Arizona and California, and have served thousands of people. I also founded several manufacturing businesses, invented a line of popular holistic medical devices and led workshops about energy medicine and healing all over the USA and abroad.

I developed chronic fatigue syndrome in my 30's and low energy prevented me from enjoying the greater success I knew I was capable of. Chronic insomnia started troubling me soon after. In spite of that I achieved a lot.

I had a big spiritual awakening when I was in Guatemala on a personal retreat and participated in healing ceremonies with local Mayan *shamans*. They helped me to see that the path I was on, although a good one, was not fully expressing the higher purpose of my life. I returned to the States determined to change my life, no matter what it took. I did more shamanic ceremonies in California and they were very intense. In one of them I felt like I was experiencing my own death. From this perspective I could see that I had not yet fully embraced my higher purpose and was living a relatively empty life. I resolved to devote myself totally to my path of being a healer.

I have always had psychic abilities and ability to facilitate, or channel, the flow of healing energies to my clients. Around that time my capacity to channel higher dimensional energies really opened up. I am now calling these energies *transmissions* since higher love and light is flowing to the people or groups I am working with.

At the time of publishing this book I am 65 years old and enjoying a miraculous life. I am staying in touch with my inner calm center, even while going through enough ups and downs to fill a whole book of its own (and probably be quite entertaining). After a long career in holistic medicine and technologies I am now doing what I am most inspired to be doing with my life – helping people free themselves from inner pain and stress so they can fulfill their most inspired purpose. I am also blessed with good physical health and can climb to the peaks of high mountains that were challenging to me in my youth. My heart has opened to enjoying the richness of relationships more than I allowed myself in my earlier years.

I now understand most of the reasons for all the suffering and struggles I went through, and some are totally different than what would be explained by conventional psychology. Some of these hidden reasons for pain and stress may likely be affecting you as well. You will gain some fascinating insights into these in the next chapters.

I have faced myself a lot, passed (and flunked) many tests and come to peace with most of my fears and insecurities. But guess what? The inner demons I struggled with in my youth have not fully gone away. I am still aware of inner pain that comes and goes. The difference is that instead of seeing it as something wrong with me I see it as an opportunity for greater self-love and compassion. I now know how to clear my own blockages and pain and use these experiences to help me be a better healer. This is in line with the truth that we are best at helping others heal from the brand of suffering we have personally experienced.

I am grateful I can share the fruits of all my searching, study and decades of clinical experience with you.

The experiences and specific challenges of your life have probably been quite different than mine. Yet I would suspect that they had a similar effect in helping you see the difference between what is important and unimportant, what fulfills you and what drains you. Life has a way of getting our attention like that!

This book is divided into four sections.

Part I: Weapons of Mass Distraction explores the "WHY" behind our modern epidemic of stress. It will give you insights and understanding of what trauma is, where it really comes from and how it may be affecting your experience. Knowledge is power. Getting clear on these things is an important key to freeing yourself and keeping your inner space clear.

Part II: From Healing Yourself to Self-Mastery contains simple, highly effective practices you can do for yourself to reclaim your calm center – even if you think you can't meditate. Even a few minutes a day of doing these practices can make a huge difference in your clarity of consciousness and quality of love in your life.

Part III: Getting Help – New Accelerated Methods for Healing Trauma contains information about new vibrational healing methods that can produce accelerated results for healing PTSD, depression, phobias and other related conditions. This section will be valuable if you need more effective support on your healing journey than you have received so far. You will learn about treatment using light therapy on acupuncture points that has permanently relieved the nightmares and flashbacks of PTSD from war veterans in one or two sessions.

Part IV: Where to Go from Here starts the conversation about how to live a passionate, fulfilling life as you are reclaiming your calm center. It also offers valuable resources for further learning.

You will get much more benefit if you read Section I first before turning to the solutions offered in *Sections II* and *III*.

Come in with an open mind on this journey.

PART I

WEAPONS OF MASS DISTRACTION

This section will give you information and insights about why our minds tend to feel so overactive and often disturbed in our modern age. Some of what you are about to read is common knowledge. Some of it may be new to you, and may challenge your belief systems.

We will start with a powerful quote from the bestseller book *The Four Agreements* by Don Miguel Ruiz. The quote describes the condition of our minds, and a major reason you may feel discombobulated and have a hard time meditating:

"Your whole mind is a fog which the Toltecs called a mitote. *Your mind is a dream where a thousand people talk at the same time, and nobody understands each other. This is the condition of the human mind – a big* mitote, *and with that big* mitote *you cannot see what you really are."* [3]

So where do those *"thousand people talking at the same time in our minds come from?* In the next chapters you will learn the answer. You are likely to find some of this information surprising.

Chapter 2: *"PTSD and the Brain"* will help you understand the ways our brains can be remodeled by trauma and stress, and how this affects our overall health and well-being.

Chapter 3: *"When Childhood is Painful"* offers a brief overview of how so many of us been programmed for PTSD in our childhoods, including some eye-opening statistics.

Chapter 4: *"Weapons of Mass Distraction"* talks about external causes of stress and how some of the entrenched powers in our society profit from amplifying your angst.

Chapter 5: *"The Dark Side of Your Mind"* will give you new insights about the hidden origins of inner blockages that have been clouding your sense of inner calm and joy.

[3] Ruiz, Don Miguel, *The Four Agreements*, Amber-Allen Publishing 1997

By understanding what has been detracting from your peace of mind you can more easily free yourself from those things.

2

PTSD and the Brain

I have a theory about the human mind. A brain is a lot like a computer.
It will only take so many facts, and then it will go on overload and blow up.
-- ERMA BOMBECK

OUR EPIDEMIC OF "LOW-GRADE PTSD"

Let's start by taking a fresh look at PTSD, or *Post-Traumatic Stress Disorder.* By understanding what PTSD is and how it may be affecting you, you will be able to better understand how and why the self-healing methods presented in this book work.

PTSD is characterized by frequent anxiety, insomnia, nightmares, social avoidance and high sensitivity to stimuli. These unpleasant experiences can be triggered by things that seem harmless and innocent to most people, such as social mixers, movies, relationship challenges and unexpected noises. These experiences bring up past traumatic experiences so intensely that the person re-lives them. Such experiences are called "triggers". Basically PTSD is reliving past traumatic events when you get triggered – whether you want to or not.

19

PTSD is now affecting people in every walk of life, not just veterans returning from war. About five million Americans suffer with full–blown PTSD that incapacitates them, and these are the ones we hear about in media coverage.[4] **Most of the rest of us experience the after-effects of trauma on a less incapacitating level. I call this "low-grade PTSD".** We can live and function, but this form of PTSD creates ongoing tension in our bodies, a negative committee in our brain that never shuts up and many brands of chronic pain, depression, anxiety and fatigue. Even these more "normal" levels of chronic stress can be quite challenging.

I believe that PTSD is not just caused by the known traumatic events that happen to us – it can also be brought on or aggravated by hidden internal stress factors that are not well understood (see Chapter Five).

Somehow the barrage of all those challenging experiences we are regularly exposed to is overloading our circuits and triggering our brains into some of the same experiences veterans of actual war are going through. With this common kind of PTSD it can be very frustrating trying to heal yourself because of the way the brain is wired. It seems that the more you try to get rid of old pain the more entrenched it gets.

A great analogy about this comes from ancient Greek mythology. Do you remember the story about the seven labors of Hercules? Hercules' second labor was to kill a fearsome monster called the Hydra. It had nine vicious, snarling heads with poisonous teeth. One of these heads was immortal. Hercules set to work trying to kill the Hydra, but whenever he cut one head off with his sword two heads would grow back in its place. He soon realized that with all his power and strength he could never kill the Hydra that way. He needed some help, so he enlisted his nephew Iolaus.

---

[4] http://www.ptsd.ne.gov/what-is-ptsd.html

INDEFESSA GERENS REDIVIVIS BELLA COLVBRIS   ARGOLIS AD LERNÆ TVNDITVR HYDRA VADVM

Iolaus used a torch to burn each severed head with fire after Hercules whacked it so it could not grow back. Hercules then cut off the final immortal head and buried it in the ground under a big rock.

So many of us have invested huge amount of time and money into psycho-therapy, workshops and oodles of healers, coaches and spiritual teachers. We have been good people and tried our best to heal ourselves and make the world a better place. Yet every time we seem to clear up one life issue it can seem that two more are growing back in its place just like the Hydra. Do you know what I mean?

In the story of Hercules he never did fully destroy the final immortal head of the Hydra, he just buried it. And as the title of the book by Karol Truman so truly states *Feelings Buried Alive Never Die*. A better way is needed than fighting or burying our inner pain or depression. That better way is accepting the pain as an opportunity for personal and spiritual growth, and then transforming it into greater love and empowerment.

We will now take a look at our marvelous brains – how they can get hijacked by trauma and stress, and how they can be re-wired back to balance and well-being.

BUGS IN OUR MINDS

Recent research has shown that our brains and nervous systems have the quality of *neuroplasticity*. That is the ability to be physically and functionally molded by repeating experiences.

As the line goes in many jokes, do you want to hear the good news or the bad news first about neuroplasticity?

OK, we'll start with the good news - neuroplasticity allows young children to learn multiple languages easily if they hear them spoken at home. It also is a major reason people who have had injuries and strokes may regain normal functioning by going through rehabilitation.

Now for the bad news. Neuroplasticity is also the reason that the brains of children in abusive families or soldiers in battle can get hard-wired to be hypersensitive to triggers of stress and develop PTSD. But wait, here's some really good news - there are new healing methods that can re-wire our brains back to more positive, life-affirming functioning. These methods can work no matter how much hell you have been through.[5]

Our brains work similarly to computers. I'm sure this is because computers were created by the human mind. Computers process information and run on programs. If the program is well-written and used properly, it can create great, rapid results that put a big smile on our face. If the program contains *bugs* (errors) or what computer geeks call *corruption*, it will cause all kinds of unpredictable problems and frustrations. And make us spend a lot

[5] See Chapter 13 for details on these new therapies. Section II gives you details on methods that are marvelous for self-clearing stress and trauma.

of time, and maybe money, trying to get the bugs fixed. Ever feel like throwing your computer against the wall?

I'm going to show you how our minds are also susceptible to bugs and "corruption" that can make us have a bad day (or miserable life), and what we need to do to stop being controlled by these negative programs.

What computers do in themselves is neither good nor bad, positive or negative. A computer simply stores and processes bits of information and regurgitates them as it is directed to do. Good information in = good information out. Garbage in = garbage out. So if you have good software loaded into your computer and use it properly, it is a thing of beauty.

That is how it is with our minds and our pure center. Feed positive, loving and empowering messages and images into it and we enjoy good and harmonious experiences in our life. Feed disturbing, manipulative and fear-based messages into it intensely enough and it will create some variation of PTSD. (tip – turn off the TV news!)

Our brains have evolved to help us thrive and survive. They are designed to protect us and keep us safe. When working properly our brains can be very efficient at helping mobilize our bodies to immediately respond to threats and danger, and then chill out and relax once it gets the all clear signal.

Unfortunately for people who have been through a lot of trauma there can be major software bugs in their brains. When trauma has been intense enough there are often actual changes in the neurological wiring of the brain that make it incapable of differentiating between a real threat and many harmless experiences. After being triggered into a stress response it is also much harder for them to go back to the calm "all clear" brain state than normal people.

This has created the agony of PTSD for many war veterans, and also for people who have been through traumatic childhood or adult experiences. PTSD is called post-traumatic stress disorder because it creates traumatic feelings and hyper-arousal that continue long after there is any real reason for it.

THE BRAIN

There are three major regions of the brain, each of which has a role in keeping us safe. The lower part of the brain is called our reptilian brain because it governs basic survival functions including hunger, thirst, sleeping and waking, crying, breathing, temperature regulation and our energy levels. Our lower reptilian brain usually does a great job of maintaining homeostasis – a healthy balance of our life functions.

The middle of our brains (midbrain) is also called the limbic system, or mammalian brain. It is the seat of our emotions and danger warning systems. This part of the brain lifts us above our more primitive life functions into our ability to navigate complex social relationships, experience pleasure and sort out our incoming perceptions. The limbic system includes the amygdala, hippocampus, hypothalamus and thalamus.

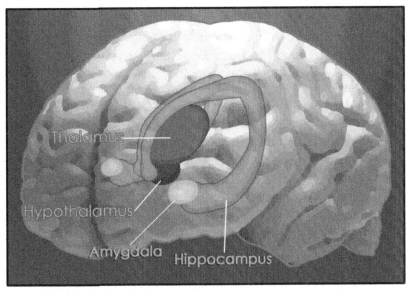

Amygdala, hippocampus and hypothalamus

When you are feeling very emotional you lose track of time. When strong emotional memories from long ago are triggered you can feel them just the same as if the original event is happening now. Many men groan about how when they get into a fight with their female partner she can bring up emotional "ammunition" from months or years ago to prove what an ass he is. In that fight it becomes as real to her as if it happened yesterday. The man is bewildered because he forgot about those experiences long ago. This of course can also happen with genders reversed and in gay relationships.

My father told me a humorous story about this kind of emotional recall. My paternal grandfather was a hard edge Polish immigrant who had a hatred for labor unions going back to days long before I was born. When he was on his deathbed and barely had enough energy to move or speak someone in his sickroom mentioned something about labor unions. Somehow my grandfather abruptly sat up and in a loud voice started sounding off about how much he detested the unions!

The upper and largest part of the brain is called the cerebrum. It is divided into a left and right hemisphere, and contains many functions that work with our sense organs, language abilities, comprehension, memory and much more. The frontal lobe of the cerebrum is the part of most interest to this discussion. This section governs our sense of empathy, putting things into perspective, planning and ability to filter our experience.

Filtering is our ability to take in what is relevant or beneficial for us and blocking out the rest. **People with PTSD often lose this filtering ability**. They become over-stimulated by many common events that don't bother most people. Mindfulness meditation has been proven to be effective for strengthening the filtering ability of this part of the brain.

The lower and middle parts of our brains protect us instinctively by sensing incoming information and creating rapid physiological changes to allow us to fight or flee. The higher brain centers are more cool and collected. They gather data to make an assessment of how to respond to situations.

The part of the brain most closely associated with PTSD is the *amygdala*, nut shaped structures in the limbic midbrain. The amygdala creates associations between common experiences of life and past hurts and fears in an attempt to protect us from encountering those same hurts again.

This is useful to an extent - it is good to remember that touching that hot plate causes an "owie" in your fingers, or that ignoring emotional red flags in potential dating partners usually ends up badly.

When the amygdala part of the brain is activated by a triggering experience it prepares the body to respond to danger. It does this by sending a distress signal to the nearby part of the brain called the hypothalamus. The hypothalamus is the major command and control center of the autonomic nervous system (ANS), the body's stress response system. The ANS is divided into two sections - sympathetic nervous system, which activates the body for action, and parasympathetic, which relaxes the body and quiets it down. Once the hypothalamus swings into action it instantly gets the body ready to fight or flee through turning on these sympathetic responses:

- Heartbeat speeds up and blood pressure increases
- Breathing deepens
- Large amounts of glucose (sugar) is released from storage in fat to increase available energy
- The adrenal glands go on high alert and start dumping adrenaline into the bloodstream for "fight or flight" response
- Sight and hearing become more acute
- Digestion is put on hold and the immune system is shut down to free up as much energy as possible for fighting or fleeing

As you can see these are highly appropriate responses when there is real danger, as they put our body in top shape for dealing with emergencies. The vulnerability of the system is that the amygdala can go on overdrive and cause us to stay in a state of fearful arousal even when there is no actual threat facing us. So it is appropriate to get riled up if a real car is swerving toward you at 70 mph. But it is not helpful if you get tense and anxious any time you are driving.

This is the dilemma and tragedy of PTSD - the amygdala of the brain gets programmed to create inappropriate associations of danger and emergency to harmless experiences of everyday life. This wires our body to be in a sympathetic stress response some or most of the time. Staying in sympathetic stress mode can be devastating to the body and is associated with these health issues:

- Heart disease
- Hypertension
- Cancer
- Immune deficiency
- Chronic fatigue
- Fibromyalgia
- Chronic anxiety and/or depression, phobias
- All kinds of digestive disorders
- Chronic pain
- Urge to self-medicate with alcohol or drugs
- Over-active mind, making it hard to be in your calm center and be happy

Sadly, our modern society is full of triggers that stimulate our stress systems much of the time.

What is the cost of all this? The first is the obvious cost in human suffering and death. The next is the massive economic cost. Expenditures for treating heart disease, cancer and anxiety disorders in the USA alone total over **$640 billion dollars a year**.

So where does all this stress really come from? **The origins of our mental and emotional stress can be roughly divided between external causes and internal causes.** The external causes are those that we take into ourselves from people around us, the media, the internet and our environment. The internal causes of stress are those that arise from inside of our own minds. Reading about these could rapidly expand your consciousness and accelerate your healing process. These will be described in the next three chapters.

We will next look at how childhood experiences may have seeded the experience of PTSD.

3

When Childhood is Painful

*Children should be seen
and not hurt*

No discussion about the causes of stress and PTSD would be complete without looking at what happened to us as children, and how it imprinted our brains, bodies and spirits.

There are already plenty of excellent books on the subject of child abuse, including the landmark book *The Courage to Heal* co-written by my sister Laura Davis.[6] Therefore I will not devote a lot of this book to repeating the same information.

Here are some meaningful statistics here that show just what a challenge child abuse is, and how it contributes to our epidemic of PTSD.

While not all adults who feel stressed and overwhelmed were abused as children, a high percentage of them have been. According to published studies more than half of all the people who seek psychiatric care have been abused as children or lived through violence in their families.

[6] Davis, Laura and Bass, Ellen The Courage to Heal, Harper Collins 2008

A famous study called ACE (Adverse Childhood Experiences) surveyed 17,421 adults between 1995 and 1997.[7]Most of these were higher income people who could afford premium health insurance through Kaiser Permanante. Of this group, 28% of the women and 16% of the men reported that they were sexually molested during their childhood, and more than 25% reported being physically abused. The study was able to track the long term outcomes of the participants, and showed that those who were molested or abused as children have experienced more financial problems, health issues and lower income as adults than people who with non-abusive childhoods.

Here is another startling statistic from the U.S. Department of Health and Human Services, Administration on Children, Youth and Families. For every soldier who is serving in a war zone there are 10 children who are being abused in their own families. A high percentage of abused children develop PTSD. This means that U.S. families create many more people with severe trauma than actual military battlefields![8]

In early childhood our emotional brain, also called the *limbic system,* became programmed. If you were fortunate enough to grow up in a loving, secure home with good interpersonal boundaries your brain got programmed with a positive, resilient view of life. People who grew up in violent or abusive families don't fare so well.

When something terrible happens to you there are three things you can do. You can fight, run away, or just space out or *dissociate.* When you are a little child you can't fight back. You could run away, and I did that when I was about 4 years old. Of course that didn't last long. So what we usually do is dissociate. When you dissociate you're not fully in your body. You protect yourself by getting out of your body so you can divorce yourself from feeling.

Imagine a girl is in her bedroom at night and hears her father or uncle or brother coming at a certain time. She has experienced

[7] https://www.cdc.gov/violenceprevention/acestudy/

[8] Van Der Kolk, Bessel, the Body Keeps the Score, Penguin Books, 2014, pgs 20-21

molestation with this person before so she knows what is going to happen. She wants to escape yet she probably depends on this person for being fed and for her safety. This creates an impossibly confusing conflict. So what she does is dissociate from her body. She is in effect saying "here's my body, but I can't stand to be in it". The same could be true of frequently battered children or adults.

When children go through this experience it literally rewires their brain. The parts of the brain that are our alarm center for danger often go onto constant alert, and secretion of stress hormones goes on overdrive (see Chapter Two). Certain centers in the brain that have to do with feeling bodily sensations and being close with other people shut down. The tragedy is that these centers of feeling and intimacy can shut down for years, decades or a lifetime. Some people are more susceptible to this permanent shutting down of brain centers than others.

The diagram below shows two brains. The upper brain represents a person who has not been through significant trauma and still has his centers open that relate to empathy and human connection. These are shown as white areas. The lower brain is of a person who has been deeply traumatized. All but one of those brain centers are shut down.[9]

---

[9] Ibid, pgs 293-294

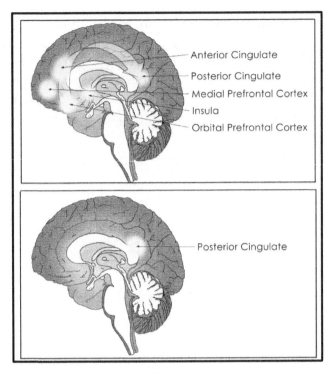

How brain centers shut down due to trauma
(Diagram used courtesy of Bessel Van Der Kolk)

Ongoing secretion of stress hormones due to feeling unsafe in the world pre-disposes people to many chronic diseases. Bessel Van Der Kolk, a preeminent researcher in the field of trauma has shown that adults who were abused as children have much higher rates of fibromyalgia, migraines, irritable bowel syndrome, asthma and many kinds of auto-immune diseases[10]. Researchers in the medical field of psycho-neuro-immunology have also found links between early childhood trauma and higher incidence of cancer.

One of the best ways to put confusing and conflicted experiences into perspective is to talk about them. Children who have been sexually molested usually feel so ashamed that they don't even want to talk about it, and if they do they are almost always told

---

[10] Ibid, pgs 293-294

"no, you're crazy, we don't talk about those things in this family" or something like that.

My older relative Mildred (name changed) demonstrated a major change in personality and life direction after what I believe was childhood abuse. I say I believe because there is no way of confirming what really happened to her. Please read this story a close relative told me about Mildred and draw your own conclusions.

In her teenage years Mildred was an attractive, healthy girl who showed signs of high intelligence and interest in life. She wanted to go to college and get a higher education. When she was 19 she developed an unexplainable stabbing pain in her vagina. Her mother took Mildred to several different doctors looking for help, but none of them could relieve her pain. They were poor, so it was not easy to do that, but her mother somehow scraped the money together. Finally after close to a year she did find one doctor who did a treatment that resolved the vaginal pain.

Mildred never ended up going to college. She married at a young age and while I was growing up she seemed to be a professional patient. She always seemed to have multiple things wrong with her – worst of which was severe back pain. Mildred ended up having several surgeries for that. She wasn't an invalid, but she was always having problems. As I got older and more conscious about trauma and healing I started to understand that Mildred had been profoundly damaged by some unspoken childhood experiences.

In discussions with my psychologist colleague Greg Nevens about Chapter 15 of this book he recounted many of his patient case histories. One of them was a woman in her 60's who was referred to him for treatment of fibromyalgia pain. After a number of pain management treatments she confided in him to say that she had been forced by her parents to go through a very painful abortion when she was a teenager. Later in life she developed multiple diseases of her reproductive organs, which had led to 3 – 4 abdominal surgeries. Dr. Nevens told me that he wondered if all of those diseases and surgeries could have been prevented if that patient had received the benefit of the highly effective PTSD therapies available now at an earlier age. We will never know for sure, but my guess is "yes".

Have you gone through traumatic childhood experiences? If so I want you to know that you can heal yourself, even if you have suffered for a long time with the after-effects of those experiences. The most important place to start is renewing your commitment to loving and accepting yourself completely and unconditionally. You can benefit from the practices and resources offered in Sections II and III of this book, even if years of previous therapies have not brought you peace and resolution.

The next chapter deals with external causes of stress, which I not so affectionately refer to as Weapons of Mass Distraction.

4

Weapons of Mass Distraction

You tell me it's the institution, well you know,
you better free your mind instead
-- JOHN LENNON

The rulers of ancient Rome knew that to stay in power they needed to keep the masses of people entertained and distracted. So in 140 B.C. they passed laws to give out cheap grain and offer circuses featuring gladiators brutally fighting each other in the Coliseum. This was how the Roman rulers appeased the lower income people so they could keep their support. Sound familiar?

Although as a nation we are more educated than most of the ancient Romans those who "rule" us – the conglomeration of massive corporations, financial institutions and the politicians they sponsor - continue this same old game. They know that a healthy, well-informed and prosperous population will take charge to create meaningful reform, meaning less power and profits for the big corporations. So they have created the modern version of bread and circuses. The objective of this game is to keep the majority of people having to work harder than ever to make ends meet, be distracted by a barrage of negative and polarized information through the media and be as stressed out as possible.

Servicing the devastation caused by chronic stress is extremely profitable to the medical, media and pharmaceutical industries. Not surprisingly, pharmaceuticals are the most profitable major industry in the USA, leading all others with a 30% profit margin. Here are some eye opening details.

THE MEDIA AND PTSD

Do you wonder why I say that the media industry profits from PTSD? If you want to see this for yourself go to your local multiplex movie theatre and watch some of the action films being produced these days. It seems that most originality, heart and consciousness have been removed from the majority of these movies. Those have been replaced by a predictable formulaic blend of long fight scenes with loud gunfire and explosions that go on and on, dizzyingly fast moving action sequences that are totally divorced from reality, special effects that overload the brain and a clear conflict of "us versus them" between the good guys and the bad guys. Yes, the people who innovate those special effects are remarkable wizards, but their visual magic is often used for negative purposes.

Last year I succumbed to my boyish desire for escapist entertainment and took my partner to the latest Star Trek movie Beyond. I was expecting a more modern version of the thoughtful, mind-opening stories offered by the original series beloved by "trekkies". The movie started out promisingly with a new, younger version of the original Star Trek crew. But it quickly degenerated into the same predictable formula of pointless violence and mayhem I just described. We were waiting for a payoff in the form of an interesting plot twist or revelation but it never came. We left the theatre feeling kind of sick to our stomach and deadened. It took over an hour of meditation for us to get back to the feeling of being connected and clear. My partner even told me "I felt cut off from my higher self" after watching the movie.

I grew up loving these kinds of sci-fi adventurous movies. Even at my more advanced age I can still enjoy action movies that touch me and help me to see a bigger reality – the real mission of science fiction. I'm not even averse to seeing some violent fight scenes if there is a valuable message in the movie, as there was in the masterful film *The Matrix* (the original movie, not the sequels, which lacked the depth and message of the first one).

What I have seen recently is that it barely matters now whether the movie (or video games) are allegedly about Star Trek, Superman, The Avengers, X-Men or James Bond. The newer versions of all these movies are mainly vehicles to attract people's attention and then dose them with a mind-numbing overload of mayhem. These sounds and images are similar to what military service people experience on a real battlefield. Even though movies and video games are only simulations the effects on the brain can be similar to real combat. There is evidence that violent, dehumanizing movies and video games have helped motivate many of the kids who committed mass shootings at schools.

Most of these action movies are targeted to the teenage or pre-teen brain. The media consumed by older people is not much better. Most adults watch daily TV news programs and violent TV series. Similar to the bread and circuses provided by ancient Roman emperors to keep the public entertained these programs fascinate the dark side of our minds and over-stimulate us. Why is this so harmful?

Watching the TV news and violent, negative programming puts you at the mercy of three influences that can increase PTSD-like feelings. They are:

  • Hearing about overwhelmingly negative news from all over the planet or fear-inducing images that you are helpless to change, day after day. This tends to create passivity and apathy, the antithesis of being an active part of the solution.

  • By continuously presenting an "us against them" picture of the world, this programming and "news" activates the reptilian, fear-based lower parts of our brain and tends to shut down the higher consciousness centers.

- The flickering light patterns of TV screens that activate stress-producing parts of our brains and nervous systems

The bigger the TV screen is, the more damaging these are!

The small screens of mobile devices can be just as insidious when they are used to communicate negative, polarizing and false information. Twitter feeds and other social medias can serve the valuable service of keeping people connected over long distances and rapidly sharing valuable information. But social medias are increasingly used to spread false information masquerading as *"news"* and to threaten and terrorize people.

The 2016 Presidential election was part of this pattern. There has never in recent history been a more polarizing, negative election process. Donald Trump appears to be a master at connecting with masses of people and stirring up their most negative fears and emotions toward each other (a form of discombobulation). Stirring up people's powerful emotions through frequent TV coverage and Twitter feeds has proven to be an effective way keep their lower brain centers on high alert and higher consciousness centers quiescent. I see this more as PTSD-inducing "weapons of mass distraction" than a useful process for choosing a new leader.

This barrage of negative, fear-inducing news and happenings has only increased since the election. Take a step back and think about this. Can you see how this is one more example of "bread and circuses"?

Our media is full of such disempowering and fear-triggering images - and we are addicted to them. We need to practice mental hygiene by being more discriminating about what messages we take into our inner garden.

At the time of writing this chapter the United States seems to be strongly polarized between the 'blue states" and "red states", the Democrats and Republicans, those who would protect the environment and those who would remove all protections and extract as much from it as possible. If you feel the call to be part of the solution please look into your heart and don't contribute to this polarization, even for seemingly good causes. You can have the greatest impact by raising your consciousness and connecting with the Self. From that place you will be guided as to what actions you can do that will really make a difference.

PHARMACEUTICAL COMPANIES AND PTSD

Want to know why the pharmaceutical industry is the most profitable one in the world? According to the Centers for Disease Control 48.7% of all Americans use at least one prescription drug.[11] Drug companies spend 19 times more on marketing and lobbying politicians than they do on research and development.[12]

Lobbyists for the big pharmaceutical companies have tremendous influence over Congress and the Food and Drug Administration. As a result many of them have government-granted monopolies on life-saving drugs, and they take advantage of this by jacking up the cost of what used to be inexpensive generic drugs by hundreds to thousands of percents.[13]

The mind-altering effects of drugs have fascinated mankind since ancient times. Almost every civilization since the dawn of recorded history has had extensive use and dependence on drugs of some kind. Each drug or herb has its proper use, when used for nutrition, healing of the body or in the context of spiritual ceremony. The recreational use of drugs is a symptom of our sense of disconnection from our spiritual source. We crave mind-altering drugs because the temporary experience of peace or pleasure they bring reminds us of the bliss of connecting with the Divine. We all remember that feeling on some level. In order to really live in that experience we need to turn within ourselves and reclaim our calm

---

[11] http://www.cchr.org/cchr-reports/psychiatry/introduction.html, also http://www.cdc.gov/nchs/fastats/drug-use-therapeutic.htm

[12] http://www.huffingtonpost.com/ethan-rome/big-pharma-pockets-711-bi_b_3034525.html

[13] See article in Life Extension magazine Extortionist Drug Prices, March 2017 issue. This information is freely available from many other sources as well.

center. When we keep depending on drugs to simulate bits and pieces of inner connection and avoid our real inner work those drugs become weapons of mass distraction. There has never been any society in the history of the human race that has gotten more distracted with drugs than the United States in recent times.

Mind-altering drugs are now routinely prescribed by doctors for a vast host of human experiences that people in the past just lived with, or received support for from their church or community. Drugs are prescribed for aggressive children, smoking, bedwetting, alleged eating disorders, learning challenges, and criminal behavior, to name a few. From 1996 to 2005 the drug industry increased their marketing of these drugs between 300 – 500%.

Since the approval of Prozac by the FDA in 1987 the use of antidepressant medications has quadrupled in the United States with 1 in 10 Americans now taking them. Women are 2½ times more likely to take antidepressants than men, and 23% of all women in their 40s and 50s use them. Most of these prescriptions are given without an evaluation by a qualified mental health professional, or an exploration of alternative therapies such as psychotherapy, cognitive therapy, EMDR or other alternative methods of treatment that could be much more effective at helping people actually resolve their conflicts and issues.[14]

Increasing numbers of research studies are showing that antidepressants are not much more effective than placebo pills (pills with no medical effects). A retrospective analysis of all FDA clinical trials for four antidepressant drugs found that they didn't perform significantly better than placebos in treating mild or moderate depression, and the benefits of the drugs were "relatively small even for severely depressed patients"[15]

14 http://www.apa.org/monitor/2012/06/prescribing.aspx also http://www.health.harvard.edu/blog/astounding-increase-in-antidepressant-use-by-americans-201110203624
15 PLoS Medicine 2008, study led by Irving Kirsc, now associate director of the Program for Placebo Studies at Harvard Medicine School

Not only are these drugs less effective than touted by those who sell them, they are also proven to increase suicide and violent behavior in many people taking them. In 2004 the FDA issued a public health advisory warning of these risks. In that same year an official from the FDA Office of Drug Safety warned that out of every 100 children put on antidepressants 2 - 3 will commit suicide. Knowledgeable doctors believe that this number is considerably understated because this statistic is based on research done by the makers of antidepressant drugs.

Eli Lilly, the manufacturer of Prozac did a retrospective study of people in Germany taking Prozac who had committed suicide. The study showed that people taking this drug were six times more likely to kill themselves than people taking placebos or older antidepressant drugs. According to investigator Peter Breggin, M.D., Eli Lilly hid these findings from the German agency and the US FDA[16].

Another disturbing trend is putting children or teenagers in foster homes or other institutions on powerful antipsychotic drugs to make more compliant with authorities. According to published articles from the American Psychological Association children in foster care are 450% more likely to receive these drugs than other children covered by Medicaid. Hundreds of these children are receiving multiple antipsychotic drugs at higher doses than are considered safe. Even some infants in foster care are receiving them[17].

At the other end of the age spectrum the big drug companies have been price-gouging seniors for a long time. The industry made 711 billion dollars in profits between 2002 and 2012 through drug purchases by Medicare. While in all other countries government health agencies negotiate with drug companies for big quantity discounts US law prohibits Medicare from seeking better pricing. In 2006, the first year of Medicare's prescription drug program the

16 http://breggin.com/?option=com_content&task=view&id=43&Itemid=66, also file:///C:/Users/TEST/Downloads/fdapressconfsept142004.pdf
17 Van Der Kolk, Bessel, The Body Keeps the Score, 2014 Penguin Books, pgs 37-38

profits of the biggest drug companies rose 34%. All of this is supported by cozy relationships between politicians, drug companies, their lobbyists and the FDA.

There is also a rising trend in prescribing these drugs for demented seniors in nursing homes to reduce alleged behavior problems, even though they are likely to create additional health problems. These include diabetes, weight gain and painful muscle spasms.

So what is the connection between the drug companies and big media conglomerates I wrote about earlier? Plenty. There have been new disclosures about business ties between drug companies and media conglomerates. For example, the *British Medical Journal* recently showed that James Murdoch, son of media mogul Rupert Murdoch worked for drug giant GlaxoSmithKline (GSK) at the time of the writing of the article. Murdoch's flagship newspaper in Australia accepted a large amount of money for publishing a series of articles to influence health policies. Media companies are controlled by corporate interests, some of which also have interests in drug companies[18].

A CONSPIRACY?

In his intriguing book *The Transfiguration of Our World*[19] author Gordon Asher Davidson uses the term the *"cabal"* to refer to the financial, political and corporate interests invested in greed and keeping the old order in place.

This cabal figured out a long time ago that if you make people feel fearful, dis-empowered and guilty, and make them believe that they are dependent on you for their protection, salvation, forgiveness, enlightenment or whatever, you can control them and gain power and money for themselves.

---

18 http://articles.mercola.com/sites/articles/archive/2011/12/18/journalism-in-drug-industry.aspx
19 Davidson, Gordon Asher The Transfiguration of Our World, Golden Firebird Press 2015

To distract people from their own depredations the cabal always needs to have an enemy scapegoat to rally the people against. During the Cold War it was the Russians, during the Vietnam War it was the Viet Cong, now the scapegoats are Islamic terrorists. There certainly are plenty of real Islamic terrorists out there. I personally believe, however that the cabal has committed far greater evil than these terrorists have done or are capable of. They have exaggerated the power of these groups to create fearful and disempowering images to fill the media.

This is what George Orwell described in his prophetic novel 1984 [20]. He described a world where there were three major countries, and each of them was in a perpetual state of war with one of the other ones. Images of the perpetual wars were constantly broadcast to the populace through television screens that were everywhere. Orwell's prophesy has now come true through the ubiquitous TV monitors found throughout homes, restaurants, bars, fitness clubs and even on the sides of buildings in some big cities.

What has been discussed in this chapter is only the tip of the iceberg. I have become aware of weapons of mass distraction that go way beyond the abuses of pharmaceutical companies and the media. These may involve insidious methods of mind control and manipulation created by the cabal that rival or exceed the plots of science fiction movies such as The Matrix. [21]

I am not going to say a lot more about the cabal, or the conspiracy to increase PTSD, depression and sickness among our populace. This is a huge subject in itself, and dwelling too much on it could create a diversion from the main message of this book. Whether or not you believe the stories our leaders and the media tell us, or that the cabal exists, it is not nearly as important as your choice to

---

[20] Orwell, George 1984, Penguin Books 1950

[21] The Matrix movie released in 1999 by the Wachovski brothers tells a masterful story about a world in which machines have enslaved the human race and are using us as energy sources while making us believe that our lives are going on as normal. While this is not literally true it is a powerful allegory about the pervasive illusions the human believes is "reality".

reclaim your calm center. You can do that regardless of your beliefs about the world. I have given you some facts and perspectives here, and encourage you to do your own research and draw your own conclusions.

HOW TO OPT OUT OF THE STRESS BASED CULTURE

Trying to "opt out" of the stress-based system has been very difficult up to now. There are two major reasons for this. The first is that we are inundated with experiences and messages that tend to reinforce and increase stress. The other reason is that most healing systems used to try to heal the mind are created by the mind. Trying to use the mind to heal the mind rarely works. This often has the effect of making the stress programs even more resistant! Kind of like using fire to fight fire, as the old expression goes.

Remember the basic principle of computers – Garbage In, Garbage Out. The mind works that way too. That which you take in determines a lot about the quality of your experience. Listen to uplifting, high vibrational music. Get out in nature and take in the beauty through all your senses as often as possible. Choose to spend time with people who love you and support your awakening. You may have already eliminated or reduced harmful items in your diet such as sugar, gluten, artificial foods and harmful chemicals. Make sure you also do that with your mental diet. This is a top way to reduce PTSD and start prettying up your inner garden.

A major principle of consciousness is that what you focus on expands. This is based on how the brain works. It is our sacred responsibility to focus our attention on sights, sounds and experiences that are uplifting, beautiful and life-affirming as much as we possibly can. This does not mean hiding from the world in a never never land. Even if you are in the thick of a challenging work assignment or serving in a refugee camp you can behold beauty and upliftment if you are doing your best to be part of a team of loving hearts at work producing a solution.

One of the deeper teachings of Buddhism is that what we call the "world" is really a projection of our minds. What this means to me is: change your mind – change your world. The best way to help restore freedom, fairness and harmony to your world is to free yourself internally, then share your love and truth with as many other people as possible.

Know that reclaiming your pure center is not just for you - it is a courageous spiritual and political act that touches and helps free all humanity.

5

The Dark Side of Your Mind – How to Understand and Come to Peace with it

Your pain is not all your own
-- DARREN STARWYNN

INTRODUCTION

Do you ever just feel funky - having unexplainable pains and concerns, or feeling depressed for no reason? Are you bothered by strange thoughts and memories that seem to come out of nowhere? Ever feel discouraged because it seems like such hard work to grow and heal and get your life where you want it to be? When you feel these things you may blame yourself. You may beat yourself up further and wallow in feelings of being a loser or a bad person.

There are real reasons you are feeling those things, and much of this has likely been hidden from your initial understanding. It is really important for you to understand these reasons, so you don't think that there is something wrong with you! The fact that you may be feeling discombobulated is not due to some fault or weakness in you, as you will now see.

Most traditional human cultures honor both the light and dark sides of life and the psyche. Because they lived close to the Earth and the cycles of the seasons, traditional people were less prone to idealize life. The Judeo-Christian religions tend more to elevate goodness and virtue and condemn and judge that which is considered dark. For example Mother Mary and various saints represent the idealized feminine nature in the Christian religion, while the darker, less controlled expressions of human nature, including sexuality, have often been labeled as sin and error.

In traditional Indian spirituality both the light and dark sides of the feminine principle have been equally honored. Hindus, for example worship both Lakshmi, goddess of love and beauty and Kali, goddess of revenge, death and sexuality[22]. Ancient Greek gods and goddesses displayed all the same vices that ordinary people did, including rage, jealousy and illicit sex. Traditional Chinese medicine and art recognizes the balance of Yin-Yang as the basis for everything in the creation. Yin represents what is cold, dark, receptive and feminine, while Yang represents heat, light, penetrating energy and masculine. There is no judgment associated with any of these qualities, they are simply varying expressions of energy.

22 http://www.scns.com/earthen/other/seanachaidh/godindia.html

Kali

Lakshmi

Our modern culture's tendency to idealize what we are taught is good and noble and to condemn and distrust the parts of our psyche labeled as dark has created painful divides within our psyche. An essential part of self-healing is learning to love and honor all parts of ourselves, welcoming them all into the heart. This chapter can help you do that by providing understanding of where the dark side of your experience came from. It is easier to have love and compassion for that which you understand.

SOME OF THE STUFF WE HAVE TAKEN ON

I cannot document or prove the truth of any of the information presented in this chapter to you. This one definitely goes out of the realm of things that can be proven to the logical mind. I have come to understand these internal causes of suffering through my decades of experience as a healing practitioner, and from teachings I believe to be true. It is not necessary for you to believe all that

49

you read here to benefit from the healing methods presented in Sections II and III.

The best way to know if anything is true for you is to tune into your "gut". Feel what your gut reaction is to each of the numbered sections below. If your gut feeling is that you don't resonate with it then let it go, it is not your truth. If you do feel a positive resonance in your gut as you read it, even to the point of your hairs standing on end, you will know that there is truth for you in it. I hope you will find reading this chapter an exciting journey of self-discovery.

In *Chapter 6, The Universal Path*, you will learn the Sanskrit term *samskara*. You will learn how it refers to deep impressions in our minds that are similar to negative software programs causing buggy behavior in a computer. According to the Buddha and many other advanced teachers of consciousness *samskaras* are at the root of our angst and suffering. For now, know that all the internal stressors you are about to read about are associated with *samskaras*. This will make more sense when you read the next chapter.

There are checkboxes after each section so you can record whether what you read in that section resonates with your gut or not. This will give you valuable practice in listening to that truthful part of yourself.

Let's now examine some of the major hidden causes of stress and inner pain.

1. Your pain is not all your own

Have you read either of Eckardt Tolle's books *The Power of Now* or *The New Earth*? [23]   In those books Tolle offered a valuable explanation of what he called our *pain bodies*. Pain bodies are mass experiences of pain and stress that are shared among groups of people with a common affinity.

[23] Tolle, Eckhardt The New Earth, Penguin Publishing 2008, The Power of Now, New World Library 2004

For example, according to Tolle there is a collective pain body for all women. This pain body vibrates with the experiences that women have been going through all over the planet. These include exploitation, rape and being forced to be second class citizens to men in many cultures. So if you are female and ever feel afraid walking down the street, experience mood swings or unexplainable depression comes out of nowhere know that that this is not all about you – you may also feeling the pain body of ALL women.

There are also collective pain bodies for all Jews, low income white males, high income white males, African-Americans, Armenians, handicapped people, Native Americans and it goes on and on. We are all tied into multiple, overlapping pain bodies.

By simply recognizing this you can stop beating yourself up about having painful feelings. When you are feeling that try to look at it with curiosity, perhaps something like this: "Hey, I'm tapping into some pain bodies today. It's so good to know that it's not all about me! I think I'll meditate or share love with others to try to help dial it back for all of us."

This information resonates with me: Yes ☐　　No ☐

2. Higher consciousness is stirring up your stuff

We are now in the midst of a global awakening. The human race is rapidly moving into a collective expanded consciousness, and much of the illusions and falsehoods we have been indoctrinated with are crumbling.

Our planet is now transiting from a focus in the 3rd dimension – the material world that is full of limitations and polarizations – into the 4th and 5th dimensions. These are realms where spiritual awareness, unlimited resources and the inter-connectedness of all life becomes our new normal. In this new Earth old experiences of greed, polarization, scarcity and pollution are transforming into the consciousness of justice, unity and universal love.

You may doubt this is really happening, because if you watch the TV news it seems that there are even more terrible things happening than ever, and the situation doesn't look anything like higher consciousness.

There certainly are a lot of difficult crises going on in our world. But did you ever think about WHY they are happening?

As we awaken our consciousness expands. As a result we can better feel the deeper love in our hearts, we can meditate more easily and sense our oneness with all life. Beautiful stuff. But as we become more aware of how we are inter-connected with all life we also become more aware of those pain bodies we are sharing with others. Before the current global awakening most people were not so sensitive to these experiences, but now we are feeling it more.

Did you know that when you have the flu the discomfort you feel is not from the sickness itself? The fever, chills, body aches, headaches or sneezes are not caused by bacteria or viruses. These uncomfortable symptoms are created by your own immune system as part of its efforts to kick the sickness out of your body. This is also true for skin rashes and pimples, which are ways our bodies push toxins up to the surface.

In the same way, so much of the polarization, ethnic conflicts, economic changes and new diseases you keep hearing about are part of a natural process of popping our collective zits to remove poisons from our earth and our consciousness. All this stuff has to come up to the surface and out in the open so it can be transformed. A necessary process, but rarely fun as we are going through it.

This is also happening on a personal level. Any old experiences (samskaras) that have been buried in your subconscious mind that you have not fully healed and loved are coming up into your brain and nervous systems for re-processing. Often faster than you would like! These experiences are often referred to as "purification" by many spiritual teachers and practitioners. Often with raised eyebrows and a hesitant laugh!

Whenever you are having such an experience you can move through it more quickly and gracefully by connecting with other people who understand it, and can support you. Prayer circles, high-level healing workshops or visits to a trusted healer can make a big difference. The practices you will learn in Part II of this book are just what the doctor ordered to help move your through purification of your samskaras with flying colors!

Also honor the needs of your body even more. When you feel these purification experiences dragging you down take extra time to get out in nature and walk or hike, get a massage, bathe in healing waters if you can and clean up your diet. The detoxification of your body mirrors the detoxification of your soul. It is wise to take care of yourself on both levels.

This information resonates with me: Yes ☐ No ☐

3. No, not just this lifetime

As I mentioned above, not all people experiencing *"discombobulation"* have had terrible childhoods. The trauma may have gone farther back than that. Based on my experiences and study I am convinced that most of us have lived though many lifetimes, and that we have brought forward many of the positive and negative experiences from those past lifetimes forward into this one.

Are impressions and memories from alleged past lives the experiences of the same person we are now, in a past incarnation? Or do they filter down from our ancestors or clan? Could they be archetypal symbols of a collective unconscious, as Jung spoke about? I don't know for sure, but whatever they are I have witnessed the powerful influence these experiences have had on myself and many of my healing clients.

Our emotional brains cannot tell the difference between trauma that happened yesterday or 30 years ago, unless we have fully resolved the old imprints. This could also be true for past life trauma. That's right – your fear of public speaking could be a throwback to an ancient time when you were stoned to death for speaking out against the local tyrant.

Past life traumas could have been heavy duty. Many of my clients and friends have had memories of being burned at the stake, tortured, exiled, killed in battle and plenty more horrific stuff. Or we may have been the ones doing those things to others. I have helped many clients clear these imprints from their bodies and minds.

Karma is the record of your thoughts and actions. We are all powerful creator beings. Karma gives us the opportunity to personally experience our own creations. To the extent that you sowed seeds of love, service, benevolence and other positive contributions in your past you have *"good karma"* and will enjoy those experiences coming to you in this lifetime. If you chose to explore the dark side (and we all did) and did dirt to people and/or animals in your past then you have some *"bad karma"* and now have the exquisite opportunity to now experience the brand of suffering you created for others back then.

None of this is intended to blame or shame you. As far as I know all of us souls who have been through the human reincarnation saga have done their best to taste all manner of the "good" and "bad", the light and the dark on our journeys. If you feel burdened by unpleasant karma the greatest thing to do is fully forgive yourself. Then forgive yourself some more. After that forgive yourself even more. Relax, it was all part of the Divine Plan.

Most of us are experiencing a mixture of good and bad karma in different areas of our lives. Do you have lots of loving, close friends but can't hold onto money? Or are you usually secure with money and material things but are plagued by recurring loneliness? Or are you a very athletic person who keeps frustratingly have your knees go out? Or any other combination of blessings and setbacks?

You may know people who seem to be having a life that full of bad experiences. For example, he (or you) may have had horrific experiences as a child and now as an adult are usually broke, on the verge of homelessness, can't hold onto loving relationships and frequently struggling with health problems. If this is the case you could be led to judge yourself or your friend as a really bad person for creating such heavy bad karma.

To find the truth requires looking deeper through the eyes of the heart. Some of the people who have made the most powerful contributions to humanity have been through experiences that looked like walloping bad karma. These souls agreed to accept much heavier lessons than most people to prepare them to take on a big purpose and mission. To fulfill this mission they needed to go through a great deal of experience in a short time – what is often called "purification by fire". So it is never right to judge yourself or others. Always love and honor yourself and your experience, no matter how easy or difficult it seems.

You don't really need a past life reading to understand your past life issues. All you need to do is look at your experience now. It's all right here (unless you already resolved and forgave the issue fully). The healing process is much the same for past life trauma as it is for trauma in this lifetime.

If you want to give yourself your own past life reading take out a notebook and pen. Reflect on the good things that have come to you easily throughout your life. Write them down, those are your good karma. Then think on the recurring pains, setbacks and challenges that have plagued you for a long time – in spite of your great efforts to change or heal them. Write those down, those are your bad karma. Voila! You have just given yourself an accurate past life reading. But it may not all be your own past lives, it could be about the next item.

This information resonates with me: Yes ☐   No ☐

4. Your inheritance from your ancestors

It doesn't stop with our own karma. Most of us are also being influenced by trickle down experiences from our ancestors (including parents and grandparents).

55

In traditional Chinese culture people following Confucianism and Taoism have venerated their ancestors and performed ceremonies to pay them back for their legacy. This is based on more than superstition. We all understand how our parents (and likely our grandparents) have affected us for good or ill. Although harder to understand with the logical mind, on a soul level we are also deeply influenced by our ancestors going way back.

If you are lucky with money and positive business opportunities come to you easily, thank your ancestors. On the other hand much of your deeper emotional angst could also be connected to them.

My recent ancestors were Jews living in Poland and Lithuania. I lost most of my European relatives in the Nazi Holocaust. I have felt the agony of the huge pain body I have shared with those ancestors and have done a great deal of personal healing to come to terms with that.

The Holocaust was not the only source of my ancestor angst however. I am also aware of generations of abuse and denigration of children and women from some of my ancestors. On the more positive side I have had some virtuous and wealthy ancestors that have helped pave the way for the spiritual openness and degree of business success I have enjoyed.

When I work with clients in healing sessions ancestral issues sometimes come up. When it is clear that this is blocking them from enjoying a fulfilling life now I help them transform these programs and cut cords with the negative aspects of the ancestors. Clients that go through this process often experience huge shifts in their lives soon afterwards.

I have noticed that it is common for one child in a family to take on the brunt of ancestral angst more than others. It has come to me many times that such clients agreed on some level to clear this heaviness from the ancestral line, and so more of it came to him. This is the basis for what is often called a *family curse* – negative ancestral energy coming down through the generations until it is finally cleared by someone who says "the buck stops here" and goes through a thorough healing process. This can be done much faster and more easily now with the new healing resources available to us.

This information resonates with me: Yes ☐ No ☐

5. Curses and implants

Long before psychologists started writing about neuroplasticity people have used it to program others for beneficial or harmful purposes. As stated earlier our minds are like computers. Good information in = good information out. Garbage in = garbage out. Until we awaken enough to claim our sovereignty we tend to take programming from other people into our inner computer.

A person who loves you and gives you frequent positive and reinforcing messages can help program you into greater experiences of confidence and self-worth. That is what loving and healthy parents do for their children. Let's call this kind of giving *blessings*.

People who want to hurt you can also program your mind with negative messages that cause pain and havoc in your life. We will call this giving *curses*.

How impactful a person's blessings or curses are is based on their *soul standing*.

Soul standing refers to an individual's level of consciousness and empowerment. While there is no rule about soul standing, it is generally true that people who have dedicated themselves to developing their consciousness through focus and self-discipline raise their soul standing. All the great spiritual teachers and masters who have touched and uplifted many people had high soul standings. Many influential people in the political or business worlds have high soul standings as well.

Unfortunately there have been and continue to be people who have raised their soul standings and used it to gain personal power or wealth at the expense of others. The curses such a person can deliver are more harmful than those coming from a less developed brute.

Curses that come from people of higher soul standing are much more devastating and could persist lifetime after lifetime. People who keep suffering with some painful or limiting condition in their life no matter how much good help they get or effort they make may be dealing with a curse. But if you have had this experience don't assume it was a curse.

The difference between karma and curses is that karma is an echo of our own past actions and thoughts while curses are a message placed on our souls by someone else. Yet they are related because the susceptibility to being cursed is probably related to negative karma. Negative karma or ancestral imprints could lower a person's self-love and self-esteem, making them more susceptible to taking in new negative messages. Kind of like how bullies in the schoolyard avoid the strong, confident kids and tend to pick on the fearful one with lower self-esteem.

Implants are related to curses. In our modern medical system it is commonplace to implant pumps, stents and artificial organs into people's bodies. Many people also accept non-physical implants into their minds and energy fields. These are another form of programming that limits a person's freedom and personal power. Implants work by creating some kind of repetitive self-sabotaging reaction or behavior within a person. **The bottom line is that implants can make sovereign beings easier to influence and control.** They often work by bringing up deep feelings of fear when a person tries to remember who they really are and over-ride the control of the implant.

It is very difficult to impossible to curse someone who is full of love because there is no receptivity to the negative imprints. It is important again to remember that we are truly sovereign beings. No one can curse us unless on some level we agree to it. Of course most people are not conscious of those agreements, so they feel like victims.

When we look within deeply enough we may find that we were the ones who placed curses and implants into ourselves. Many souls have done this in a desperate attempt to ensure that they would stay safe by never again rising to a position of high spirirtual or material power. They did due to deep memories of suffering seemingly associated with mis-using power in the past and suffering severe consequences. I have discovered this to be a common pattern among healers and holistic health professionals. As with all such conditioning, these self-created limitations can be erased.

Just as the mind can be programmed with a curse or implant it can be de-programmed and freed. Both of these are part of the technology of consciousness.

This information resonates with me: Yes ☐   No ☐

6. Vows

Many people who experience recurring blockages to financial success, or inability to be in loving relationships may be experiencing the consequences of having made vows in the past.

A vow is a powerful declaration made by a person with passion and intensity. A vow has the ability to program you on a deep soul / subconscious level. For example if you are a man in love with a woman you could tell her that you love her and want to always be with her. Yet this declaration may not be powerful or focused enough to create a vow. For most people once their "in love" feelings change they could leave that person and move onto a new relationship.

If that same man summoned all his passion and focus in declaring his love he could create a much more powerful vow that would not be so easy to let go of. I have worked with clients who could not get into a satisfying intimate relationship no matter how much therapy they went through or effort they made. When I looked at these clients I could see that they were often interesting, attractive people with a lot to offer. Yet some ongoing blockage was stopping them from making the connection they craved. Sound familiar?

In many cases we found that this person had created a vow. In this or a past lifetime he may have been so bonded with a romantic partner that he summoned all his passion and creative power and declared "I will always love you forever and never be with another woman (or man)". If done with sufficient intensity (and passionate love is intense) that could create a binding vow upon his soul. Another variation are people who entered monastic orders where they took a powerful vow of celibacy or poverty, or both and it stuck lifetime after lifetime.

Happily I have seen clients free themselves from these past vows and go on to be more successful with love or money. It usually requires the presence and support of an experienced facilitator to guide them through the vow breaking and cord cutting process.

This information resonates with me: Yes ☐   No ☐

7. Chaos precedes higher order

If you are feeling like you are going through a lot of destabilization and chaos it could be a sign you are on the fast track to enlightenment! The science of physics bears this out.

A Russian physicist named Ilya Prigogine won the Nobel Prize in 1977 for his theories of non-equilibrium thermodynamics in open systems. An open system is any system that shares energy and information with its environment. That makes we human beings open systems.

One of his Prigogine's conclusions is very relevant to this discussion. He showed that as any open system raises up to a higher level of energy it goes through a period of chaos and collapse. This is part of the process of re-organizing at the higher level.

I have news for you – you ARE rapidly moving into a higher level of love, consciousness and awakening. The crazy stuff you may be going through is part of that chaos Prigogine talked about that precedes a higher level of organization. See, you are right on track!!!

This information resonates with me: Yes ☐   No ☐

CLEARING AND TRANSFORMING ALL THIS STUFF

The practices offered in Section II are potent tools for transforming the shadow side of the mind. Your commitment to do these practices, even starting with a few minutes a day could brighten your experience beyond your belief.

The next chapter entitled *The Universal Path* lays out the proven principles for clearing samskaras as taught by the great world teachers. It also includes insights and tips from my own path that I believe will make this information easier to relate to and put into practice. The chapters after that give you detailed instructions for simple practices for clearing inner pain and taking you into your calm centre. I have provided an 8 week program you can follow that will take you far in freeing yourself from old "gunk" and getting happy.

SUMMARY

I hope that what you read in this chapter helps you understand more about the nature of the inner mental fog (the *mitote*) that Don Miguel wrote about in his book *The Four Agreements*[24]. Now you know where the heck those "thousand people talking in your head at the same time" that he wrote about may be coming from. Yet you actually don't need to take any of it personally! Here is one more quote from his book that shows you that shouldn't even take your own thoughts personally:

[24] Ruiz, Don Miguel, The Four Agreements, Amber Allen Publishing 2011

"You don't need to take whatever you hear in your own mind personally. The mind has the ability to talk to itself, but it also has the ability to hear information that is available from other realms… The mind lives in more than one dimension. There may be times when you have ideas that don't originate in your mind, but you are perceiving them with your mind. You have the right to believe or not believe these voices and the right not to take what they say personally"

I do agree with this quote and believe that much of the negative voices we hear in our heads are not really us and can come from other places.

How each of us deals with the burden of gunky samskaras in our minds varies. Until we stop running from ourselves and commit to our inner path most of us have a "drug of choice" to try to keep discomfort at bay. Among the Millennial generation (ages 18 – 35) heavy drinking, intense work-a-holism, addiction to digital devices, superficial hook-up relationships, apathy or use of street drugs are mainly where it is at. People in my Baby Boomer generation (currently ages 52– 71) abuse substances less, mainly because our aging bodies can't handle them anymore. Those that I know turn more to self-help books, spirituality, volunteer work, holistic healing treatments and staying very busy. These are certainly healthier alternatives to drunken partying. Yet all of this is often used to avoid facing our own pain and doing our necessary inner work. Therefore any of this could continue to multiply *samskara*.

So let's get it straight – whether your drug of choice is marijuana or meditation the deeper healing you crave won't happen until you do the real inner work that is needed. Your real inner work starts when you stop running from your own painful feelings. It happens as you commit to relentlessly loving and forgiving yourself and others.

YOUR ASSIGNMENT OF LOVE

I feel that the most enlightened way to view the recurring issues and challenges each of us struggle with over long periods of our lives is to see it as our assignment of love. On a soul level we volunteered to paratroop into this physical reality to bring our love and spiritual power for healing a chunk of our family's, or humanity's collective suffering. We volunteered to do this to help make the world a better place. How do we know what chunk of humanity's pain we have taken on? Simple! It would be the very things that push our buttons the most and require our maximum love, patience and compassion. It would be related to some combination of the eight internal influences I described in this chapter.

I know, easy to say and can be hard to do. But how hard it seems to do depends on our state of consciousness. In the "normal" consciousness of this world it is crazy hard not to take things personally. But when you are staying in touch with your calm center it is much easier to let stress slide off your back, like the proverbial water off a duck's back.

It may seem that I have painted a very dismal picture in these last two chapters by showing all the external and internal influences that can make it seem so hard to be at peace and feel good. I'm not going to leave you hanging there! The next Section contains simple, proven practices that really work to free yourself. They work because as we clarify and uplift our consciousness we can break the taboo in our society against knowing who we really are. As we learn to let go of the gunk and identify with our true Self the abundant love in our hearts becomes our primary experience.

Before we go there here is a vital starting point for your personal journey of healing that makes it much more inspiring and fun. That is that your true Self already is pure and perfect. That Self already is free of all the influences described in this chapter and always has been. It is actually the "you" that is most real. This is the eye of the hurricane – the point that is always peaceful in the midst of the monkey mind and all the happenings of the world.

Experiencing and integrating with the part of you that is already pure and perfect is your short cut to inner peace. It's like the art of "fighting without fighting" that Bruce Lee demonstrated in his movie *Enter the Dragon*. Much less processing and angst and much more love and fulfillment. Sound good?

Informal Survey

∞

If you checked one of the Yes or No checkboxes under each of the 8 internal factors described above, I would love to know how you scored it. If you want to play please send me an email at info@drstarwynn.com and let me know how many Yes and No checkboxes you checked off – or any other comments you have about this information.

PART II

FROM HEALING YOURSELF TO SELF-MASTERY

Spiritual 'exercise' keeps your mind in shape
the way physical exercise keeps your body in shape.
-- MARIANNE WILLIAMSON

In this section you will learn techniques and guided meditations for reclaiming your calm center and increasing your joy of life. These methods take advantage of the neuroplasticity of your brain to literally rewire you back to inner balance and vitality.

I have used every one of these practices myself, and am only sharing these because these really work. If you need additional support you will find information in Section III about new clinical methods for healing emotional pain and PTSD that you can receive from professional practitioners.

I have created videos to guide you through many of the self-healing practices described here. See Appendix 2 for access information.

HERE IS WHAT YOU WILL FIND HERE

Chapter 6: *The Universal Path*, offers insight into the path of consciousness and self-healing. It is valuable to read this chapter first because it will give you greater insight into the purpose and value of the practices that follow. If you are eager to dive in and start your inner work you can skip ahead to the following chapters, and then come back to this one when you are ready for a deeper understanding.

Chapter 7: *How to Do the Practices* introduces the practices and offers some very useful guidelines and insights.

Chapter 8: *8 Week Practice Plan* contains a suggested scheduled program for moving through the practices in a progressive step-by-step way.

Chapter 9: *Body Energy Hook-Up* is a very short one that gives instructions for a simple and extraordinarily powerful technique you can combine with all the other practices

Chapter 10: Mindfulness. This is awareness of the Now moment that has been proven in numerous studies to help people transform trauma into increased tranquility

Chapter 11: *Clearing Your Inner Space* will support you in clearing and freeing up your inner garden of consciousness so you can more easily enjoy your calm center

Chapter 12: *Reclaiming Your Calm Center* teaches three of the most simple and effective and conscious breath practices

Chapter 13: *Self-Love and Forgiveness* is about the #1 experiences people need to heal

Chapter 14: *Unified Field meditation* offers a practice for experiencing connection with the totality of your Self

6

The Universal Path to Inner Peace: A Technology of Consciousness

---

Believe nothing. No matter where you read it, or who said it, even if I have said it, unless it agrees with your own reason and your own common sense.
-- BUDDHA

Inner peace?

These words have often become thought of as a trite phrase that few people take seriously. More food for a Sunday church sermon or New Age book cover than something we can experience for real.

The main reason "inner peace" has developed a bad rap is that there have been loads of teachers sharing misleading or incomplete information about what it takes to really have it. Of course there have also been many teachers who have provided the clear, straight stuff. As a result so many people have gotten confused or discouraged and put the whole subject on the back burner.

This chapters that follow introduce a series of simple internal practices that help you clear the discombobulation and pollution from your inner mind so you can enjoy your calm center. I am calling this a **technology of consciousness** because none of it involves a dogma or irrational belief system. Everything presented here can be tested and proven out within the laboratory of your own body and awareness. Please don't believe anything you read here! Put these understandings, and the practices that follow to the test and experience the results for yourself.

This section contains a roadmap to true inner peace. I did not create this roadmap – it has been charted over thousands of years by a series of master teachers and meditators who did diligent research and development in the realm of consciousness. This is a golden path that has been proven to dissolve the roots of misery and suffering and take you into the pure love and peace of your calm center. I am calling it the universal path because it is the essence of what all these great teachers worldwide have taught for creating that outcome.

Even the 12 Steps of Alcoholics Anonymous (AA) basically follows the universal path. That is why it has proven to be the most successful program for helping alcoholics get and stay sober.

The meditative practices taught in this section are all aspects of the universal path. Reading this chapter first will help you understand how the practices all fit together. When you start to do meditative practices outside of this context of understanding it is less likely that you will gain the full benefits. That is because you may be less inspired to do what it really takes to realize those benefits. You do not have to read and digest everything in this chapter to get started with the practices, however. Work through it gradually if you need to. There are deep principles here that you may want to read several times to deepen your understanding and awaken your inner knowing.

7 KEYWORDS FOR THE UNIVERSAL PATH

Here are updated definitions for some vital words for understanding the universal inner path. Some of these may be new to you and some are likely to be familiar. Regardless of whether you think you already understand any of these terms please read this with *"beginner's mind"*. That means that you leave all preconceptions at the door and read as if you are doing so for the first time. The meaning and implications of each of these words is profound. Some are in English and some are in Sanskrit because there is no adequate English translation. Those are in italics, followed by the closest approximate meaning in English.

Each of these keywords refers to an experience. They are listed in an approximate sequence of unfoldment, like steps on a path. This idea will be developed further in the section below entitled **Putting it All Together.**

I will do my best to describe these terms in a straightforward manner so your logical, left brain can be fed with clear understanding. These are all scientific terms that are part of the technology of consciousness. Allow

Have You Been Traumatized in a Religious Family?

ॐ

If you grew up in a family in which you associated Jesus, Buddha or any spiritual words with feeling abused or repressed you may recoil from hearing anything about those names here. Please know that I am not speaking about any religious beliefs or dogmas here. This is only about the pure experience of inner liberation that these teachers brought when they were alive and teaching their students the universal inner path. This is a far cry from the religions that were later founded in their names. It is my sincere request that as you read this chapter you avoid associating what you read here with any beliefs or experiences from your past. Read it with a fresh, open mind to get the best results.

73

your imagination to also flow freely as you take them in. In this way both your reason and your intuition will guide you into having your **own** insights. That's what it's all about!

The keywords are:

- *Samskara* (subconscious conditioning – mental gunk)
- *Vairagya* (disillusionment)
- *Dharma* (living your true path, the art of living)
- Purification (cleansing the gunk from your mind)
- *Annicha* (impermanence)
- Equanimity
- Enlightenment

1. Samskara or Sankara

Samskara can be approximately translated as "impressions" or "conditioning" that pollutes our subconscious minds and makes us suffer. Every negative reaction and every traumatic experience that has not been healed creates a samskara. Just as computer viruses and malware mess with the proper functioning of your computer samskaras can create all kinds of unwanted experiences through our minds. These could include stress, anxiety, insomnia, relationship problems, financial struggles, susceptibility to chronic pain, depression and a host of psycho-somatic diseases.

The universal path is the effective way to remove samskaras so your mind can be purified and relieved of suffering. The closest English phrase I can think of to describe the mass of samskaras we carry is *"mental gunk"*. This has a similar meaning to what Don Miguel Ruiz called the *mitote* (fog).

All of the internal causes of pain and stress described in Chapter Five are aspects of samskara. This chapter starts the good part, the solution to cleanse our mind of samskara so we can more easily enjoy our calm center and be happy.

Here is some valuable intel: as you persist in the practice of meditation your mind will go into an auto-clean cycle. It will start to release old samskaras. That is because when you meditate you create a clear space where you are not producing new ones. As these old samskaras come up to be released you may feel them more acutely for a short time. This could take the form of bodily discomfort, old memories you have not thought about for years, disturbing dreams or emotional upsets. This is where good guidance is crucial. These experiences actually mean that you are succeeding in meditation and that it is working for you! See the section below on purifying the mind for more understanding on this vital point.

Since this can all sound pretty abstract I will share my own striking experience. I recently attended a 10 day silent *Vipassana* meditation retreat[25]. That's right – we maintained silence for all but the last half day and sat in meditation for over 10 hours a day, with many breaks. I was sleeping in a spartan room with two roommates. When I tried to go to sleep on the third night of the retreat my heart was pounding most of the night and my feet were cramping involuntarily. As a results I got very little sleep. When I did finally sleep for a few minutes here and there I had powerful, bizarre dreams full of strong emotions. These included being in Poland when the Nazis came to take my family away to the concentration camps, a friend raging at me and more.

I was worried I was on the verge of a heart attack or stroke and was considering leaving the retreat early to get checked out in a hospital. The next day I asked to have a short audience with the teacher (we were allowed to speak during these private audiences). I expressed my concerns to him. He told me that he had led these retreats for years and it was very common for people to manifest all kinds of symptoms of sickness, pain and emotional imbalance, and that these had always disappeared by the end of the retreats. He suggested that these symptoms were signs that the meditation practice was working.

---

[25] See Resources section for more information about Vipassana meditation retreats

I was reassured enough to stay, and continued to have many unexpected memories, feelings and varied experiences arise and disappear as I meditated. On Day 10 we were encouraged to start talking to each other to break the silence. My roommates and I finally got to introduce ourselves to each other, and they told me that on the 4th night of the retreat I had sat up in bed in the middle of the night and starting loudly speaking in a strange foreign language! I don't know any foreign languages, so that was truly bizarre.

By the time I left the retreat I felt light and clear, like some deep housecleaning had happened in my psyche. Now, several months later I have noticed many positive shifts. Several new clients signed up with me the week I got back. Some holdbacks in my relationship with my partner rapidly eased. My meditation practice has certainly deepened. I credit these to the many hours of meditation that helped me release lots of samskaras that had been burdening my mind for a long time. I have no doubt I have taken a very positive step on my path of *Dharma*. Of course there are many more steps to go, and this experience has encouraged me to keep taking them.

It is vital to know that no one else can MAKE us accept pollution into the sacred temple within our minds. At some point we have to agree to accept it. This is because in truth we are sovereign beings, at full choice in our own destinies. We can be deceived and manipulated into accepting this gunk however, and that is what often happens.

2. *Vairagya*

Vairagya is probably the only thing that will actually motivate you to make the necessary efforts to be on the universal path. After all, who in their right mind would want to discipline themselves to sit in meditation, clean up old negative habits or face their s--t? Only someone who knows there is no other way they can free themselves from suffering.

Vairagya refers to the experience of deep disillusionment we fall into after looking for love and satisfaction outside ourselves and being repeatedly disappointed or humiliated. Vairagya eventually strikes us after we have spent many frustrating years "looking for love in all the wrong places". AA, which is famous for coining lots of clever phrases, teaches that people must reach "incomprehensible demoralization" before they will take the first step of recovery. That is certainly describing vairagya!

Here is a schematic that shows how we come into the experience of Vairagya:

> **We are ignorant of our connection and one-ness with universal source so...**
>> **so we search for love and satisfaction outside ourselves**
>> **inevitable disappointment sets in and brings us into**
>>> **vairagya which gives us...**
>>> **motivation to practice the universal path**

In traditional Indian culture, people would go through this process, experience vairagya and then leave their families and renounce the world so they could live a spiritually focused life apart from society. That was called being a renunciate or sanyasin.

Being a renunciate in that way is not appropriate or useful for most of us in modern Western cultures, at least not for long periods of time. I would like to propose a new version of vairagya for we modern people. That is to be impacted by enough life experiences to gain the deep understanding that true love, satisfaction and fulfillment only lie within. This then motivates us to practice the universal path to purify our minds WHILE we are engaging in our relationships and careers. This is a form of inner renunciation of illusions while actively living our *Dharma* (see below for explanation of this term).

I don't know about you, but my *Dharma* path involves taking on quite a few challenging projects, being in an intimate relationship, multi-tasking with digital devices, keeping in frequent touch with my family and offering some of my time and money to help deal with some of the pressing challenges of our society. None of that would be served by me living in a monastery[26].

This new version of vairagya may not be as easy as leaving society to live in a cave or monastery. There is no step by step instruction manual to tell us how to successfully do this! As already stated, we need to research what works for us by going within and patiently observing the way things really are. The initial pain and disappointment that drives us into vairagya eventually becomes the foundation for our wisdom and inner peace.

To be very specific, it is vairagya that will help you concentrate your mind in meditation. I have found that during my meditation practice my mind will keep wanting to think about things I am excited about or things I am worried about. Only my depth of vairagya allows me to not take either one so seriously.

3. *Dharma or Dhamma*

This word has been used in many spiritual traditions. The most ancient meaning of *Dharma*[27] and the most useful one for us now is "the path for living in harmony with Universal law".

Universal law is how the universe works. Physicists, astronomers and the like spend their lives studying the external, physical ways the universe works. Metaphysicians and meditators explore the nature and laws of consciousness, our inner universe. If we want

[26] But it is super useful to periodically have retreats where you can live like a temporary renunciate. See further information in the Resource section at the end of the book.
[27] Brereton, Joel P. (December 2004). "Dhárman In The Rgveda". Journal of Indian Philosophy. 32 (5-6): 449–489.

to lose our anxiety and enjoy inner peace we need to live in harmony with the laws of our inner universe, our true Self. We need to do the research and development within the laboratory of our own experience to find out what really works to purify our consciousness and get happy. That is our Dharma.

It is likely that as you live your Dharma you will find yourself wanting to be kind, responsible and interested in making others happier and healthier. These urges will then come from within yourself, not from externally imposed guilt-ridden belief systems. Far better!

There is one major difference between living Dharma and the ways of most religions. Most religions teach their followers to live a virtuous life because if they do they will go to heaven or paradise sometime in the future, usually after they die. A path of Dharma, on the other hand must give positive results in the here and now as you practice it, not only in the future.[28]

4. Purification

Purification is a big deal in science. For your mobile phone to work many substances had to be mined from the Earth, processed and purified to remove residues of other, unwanted chemicals. Only then could they be manufactured into the precision electronic components that make your phone do its thing. The gasoline you put in your car results from many stages of purification of crude oil.

The universal path involves purifying our minds. The impurities that need to be removed are engrained fear, trauma, disconnection, self-centeredness, anger, doubt and the like. This does not mean that our human feelings should be seen as impurities. Passing emotions of fear, anger and grief are normal and healthy. It is only when they turn into recurring, obsessive software programs in the

---

[28] For an excellent discussion of *Dharma* and the basis for *Vipassana* meditation listen to the 4 CD set The Art of Living by William Hart and S.N. Goenka. Pariyatti Digital Media, 2004

computer of our subconscious minds that they become a blockage to our growth. That is the essence of low-grade or full-blown PTSD[29].

The universal path is the effective way to systematically remove these impurities from your mind so you can experience increasing degrees of enlightenment. It involves bringing your attention within yourself in a way that allows these negative programs to be permanently deleted.

5. Annicha

This Pali term refers to the impermanent nature of our world. It is the recognition of this that drives us into vairagya – eventually discovering that there is nothing that we can depend on for happiness or security in the outside world.

While *Annicha* is a nice spiritual philosophy it is much more useful as an actual experience you have in your practice of meditation. As you meditate on the sensations in your body you will notice that they are in constant flux. Observing and deeply understanding this helps you to gain wisdom. You eventually get that there is nothing to latch onto but pure consciousness itself.

As you internalize your understanding of the impermanence of all things it is much easier to face life without anxiety. This is one of the great benefits of meditation.

6. Equanimity

Great! Back to an English word that is easier to explain. Cultivating equanimity of mind through practice is a vital key to inner peace. Equanimity means that you learn to stay grounded within the truth of your true Self and dial back your reactions to what is happening around you. I sometimes use the more modern term "becoming unfreakable" to describe equanimity.

[29] See Chapter Two for more about PTSD and the mind

Meditation is the perfect way to practice and develop equanimity. As you meditate you will sometimes have pleasant, peaceful feelings or visions. Sometimes you will feel ancy, agitated or anything but peaceful. You develop equanimity by continuing with your meditation technique regardless of either one.

7. Enlightenment

In the technology of consciousness enlightenment is the process of lightening up the density and burdensome load of the mind so we can better experience our own true divine nature.

As described in Section I our minds often resemble a hurricane. No matter how many turbulent thoughts are swirling the peaceful eye at the center of the hurricane is always present. In the same way enlightenment is not about creating a new experience of inner peace. It is the outcome of purifying the mind and body so we can more readily enjoy the experience of our true Self that has always been there.

Your true Self is already full of love, light, forgiveness, wisdom, abundance and all other good things. So as they say when the dinner bell is being rung, "come and get it!"

GAUTAMA'S SUCCESSFUL RESEARCH STUDY

One of the greatest scientists of consciousness in history was a man named Siddhartha Gautama who was born in India over 2500 years ago. Gautama did something no one had done before him – discover a reliable method by which human suffering could be relieved at its deepest core, and then effectively teach this method to many thousands of people. He was able to discover this method by going deep within himself, using his own mind and body as his laboratory.

The young Gautama grew up as a prince of a great kingdom in India. His father was grooming Gautama to succeed him as the next king, and kept him confined into a walled palace where the prince would only see people who were young and healthy. When Gautama was a teenager he slipped away from the comfort and wealth of his home and went out among the common people outside the garden walls. He started witnessing their suffering in the form of disease, old age and death. Gautama then resolved to leave his privileged life and seek the solution to human suffering.

He spent a long time exploring various ascetic and meditative spiritual paths that existed at that time. After many years of intense practices that reduced his body to skin and bones he had developed excellent powers of concentration but was not much closer to real enlightenment.

Gautama then made a stand that helped transform the world. At the age of 35 he planted himself under a tree, put himself into a meditation posture and resolved that he would not move or leave that spot until he was enlightened. In this context he was determined to discover the root causes of suffering within himself and the practical solution to it that none of his previous practices had provided.

Gautama sat under that tree without moving for seven days and nights and deeply explored the reality of his body and its sensations and reactions. He sat there until he fully experienced and understood how the mind, the body and consciousness works. While Gautama sat in his meditation vigil he was threatened by a succession of terrifying demons, and then seduced by a succession of beautiful angelic light beings. He passed these tests by staying in equanimity and not giving his attention away to any of them. Finally his process was complete and he emerged as the Buddha, the enlightened one.[30]

The Buddha spent the remaining 45 years of his life teaching people in northern India and eventually created a movement that

[30] Jesus went through a very similar process when he sat in the desert for 40 days and nights in his own silent vigil. It was reported that he was also tempted by a version of the wrathful demons and seductive angels that the Buddha faced, and he also passed the test. This seems to be a universal experience of highly evolved world teachers. Each of us has to go through our own modified version of this on our path.

has since touched many millions of people. The Buddha created a Noble Eightfold Path that gave a roadmap for people to learn the art of living and inner peace. This was his roadmap for Dharma – living in harmony with the Universe. When asked to simplify his path even further, he boiled his eightfold path down to three basic activities:

1. Stop doing any activities that harm others and yourself

2. Engage in activities that benefit and bless others and yourself

3. Purify your mind in meditation

In modern jargon the Buddha was basically saying: "Look, here's the deal – if you stop creating pain, do lots of good and clean up your inner act you will hit the jackpot of an enlightened, fulfilling life and a peaceful mind."

Jesus was another one of the great world teachers. If you bypass the belief systems created by church fathers after his death and read the actual words of Jesus you will see that his teachings were very similar to that of the Buddha. He taught "You shall know the truth and the truth will set you free[31]". Jesus was not referring to a truth of religious belief systems – he was referring to the truth of people's own experience. The art of living he taught was very similar to the Dharma of the Buddha.

Before going further, I want to make it clear that this chapter is NOT about the myriad variations of Buddhism, Christianity or any other religion. Any "ism" is based on a belief system that large numbers of people subscribe to. The real teachings and example of the Buddha was NOT about creating a new belief system. It was a set of scientific instructions to help individuals personally EXPERIENCE the reality of what relieves suffering and brings happiness. In fact, according to one leading teacher of Dharma I recently studied with none of the sects of Buddhism that proliferated in modern India have preserved the Buddha's actual

---

[31] The Bible, John 8:32

teaching – they have all morphed it into sets of rites, rituals and belief systems.[32]

Having made that clear, let's take a look at the Buddha's three recommended activities with a fresh eye. These are all vital parts of the universal path for each of us.

1. Stop doing any activities that harm others or yourself

This is simply being in reality. The reality is that we are all connected. Whenever we harm someone else we are being harmed first and foremost. When a person harms another he is literally putting himself into some degree of hell.[33]. If the harm is small, the hell will be minor, like being in a bad mood, feeling guilty or needing to be on the phone for hours with customer service. If the harm is big so will the self-created hell be.

There are two main reasons that so many people continue to do harmful things to others in spite of these consequences. Those are:

A. They are so unconscious and cut off from their heart and soul that they are already in hell. Therefore adding more hell on top of the hell they are already in is not so noticeable.

B. There is a seeming time delay between doing the harmful activity and experiencing the hellish consequences. Some people and corporations doing hurtful actions might not have their hell catch up to them for years, decades or lifetimes. But this delay factor is rapidly diminishing due to the accelerating "instant karma" that John Lennon sang about.[34]

Acting harmfully creates more discombobulated, conflicted thoughts and emotions and increases samskara. Those fill our inner temple with pollution, leaving no room for peace, calm and

32 Goenka, S.N. Meditation Now, Pariyatti Publishing, 2002

33 This is the hell we experience while being alive in our bodies, not some alleged place we go after we die

34 Instant Karma was first released as a single during Lennon's life then included in Lennon's posthumous Live in New York album, released 1986

abiding love. This takes us 180 degrees AWAY from purifying our mind and liberating ourselves from suffering.

We can call harming others "acting out". What is often harder for us to stop is hurting ourselves, or "acting in". As part of our modern epidemic of low-grade PTSD one commodity that has gotten very scarce is self-love. Lack of self-love breeds all manner of self-sabotage, self-hatred, self-condemnation and the like. Few people I know go around intentionally harming others, but plenty of them engage in thoughts and actions that harm their own peace and happiness. You will find valuable help in boosting your self-love in Chapter 13. Easy or hard, it is essential to learn to love and forgive ourselves in order to reclaim our calm center.

2. *Engage in activities that benefit and bless others and yourself*

On the positive side, whenever you bless others with caring and kindness you are being blessed first and foremost. You are receiving the greatest blessing as you love and serve others. The Moody Blues got it right when they sang

"When you stop and think about it, you won't believe it's true, that all the love you've been giving has all been meant for you." [35]

When we attune to a higher state of consciousness these truths are much more apparent. It is much easier to meditate and enjoy your calm center when your consciousness is elevated. So those who find it hard to concentrate their minds in meditation can start by following these first two activities. Again, these are universal truths that no valid religion or spiritual path would deny.

3. *Purify your mind*

When I ask people I know about meditation, including many highly conscious sorts, most of them tell me it is very hard for

35 From the Moody Blues song Question, on album In Search of the Lost Chord, 1970

them to quiet their minds and meditate. Or they say they meditate when they paint, hike, listen to music, watch sunsets, listen to guided meditation apps, etc. but find it hard to sit down without any outer stimulation and put all their attention within themselves.

If this is true for you it simply indicates that you have your work cut out for you in lightening the burden of samskaras that have polluted your deep mind. We all do.

At the beginning of this chapter you read that lots of well-meaning meditation teachers and yoga instructor have delivered misleading information to people about meditation. Let's straighten this out now.

The reason so many people have become discouraged in trying to meditate is that they were led to believe that they could sit down, breathe deeply, relax their bodies, focus on their chakras, visualize angels, chant mantras and so on and they would gain lasting inner peace. Yes, it is true that any of these activities can lighten up the surface layer of the mind and make you feel better temporarily. But did you notice how quickly that annoying monkey-like mind regenerated after the meditation class, just like the assassin from the future in the Arnold Schwarzenegger movie *Terminator 2?*[36]

The key practices the Buddha offered for purifying the mind was to practice regular meditation by focusing the mind on the breath (respiration) or the changing sensations throughout the body. From what I understand these were the key practices he used to attain his own enlightenment, and the ones he taught to his close disciples.

By observing these experiences over and over one learns from personal experience that life is really a series of sensations that are constantly changing (Annicha). This form of meditation is called *Vipassana*. The literal translation of Vipassana is to "see things as they really are."[37]

---

[36] A movie directed by James Cameron, 1991

[37] According to the Buddha's teachings meditating on the natural flow of breath and sensations in the body (*Vipassana*) is able to purify the deepest level of the

The Buddha taught that unawakened people are constantly reacting to the pleasant and unpleasant sensations of life by going into craving and aversion in relation to them. Here's the key problem – each time we react with craving or aversion to any experience we create a new samskara. In modern vernacular that means going deeper into the doo-doo! This is the opposite of liberating ourselves from suffering. The world is in the mess it is in because most of its human inhabitants do not understand this truth – including most people who consider themselves religious or spiritual.

By the way, moving out of craving does not mean that you stop having desires! Desires are a powerful, important part of our experience. The distinction is that craving comes from a place of emptiness and lack while healthy desires can be a positive celebration of being alive. Desire is the seed that creates all our positive manifestations.

One reason that mindfulness, *anapana*, Unified Field and other meditative practices that follow in this section are so powerfully effective is that they all help us move out of reaction into equanimity of mind.

ACCEPTING TEMPORARY DISCOMFORT

As mentioned above in the definition of samskaras, experiencing temporary discomfort as you commit to a meditation practice is usually evidence that you are succeeding at it! You are getting free by effectively deleting old painful programs from your inner computer. The rub is that you usually need to experience the gunk

---

subconscious mind so that *samskaras* can be released. This is what leads to true equanimity and enlightenment. The Buddha taught that more common meditations and spiritual practices in which one meditates on something external or not natural to them, such as mantras, visualizations or goddesses only works on the more superficial level of the mind. While such practices can relax and sooth temporarily and touch the heart they are much less effective for permanently liberating the mind. In modern times such practices would include meditating with recorded guided meditations via DVDs and apps.

as it is releasing out of your body/mind. This is the truth that should be shared more often by meditation teachers. They should not give the false expectation that the process of meditation and self-liberation is all about love, peace, hugs and rainbows. It can often seem like hard work, and like all important work requires dedication, patience, persistence and inspiration to keep going. The rewards of this work however, are endless.

Here's a funny fact - we really get this thing about accepting temporary discomfort in other areas of our lives. Think about it – most Americans totally understand that in order to have a strong body or fit into those slim jeans they will need to push themselves to work out or sweat in a Zumba class. Many people who want to look younger or better in bathing suits are glad to undergo painful surgeries, injections, peels and much more. Athletes and military trainees accept the rigors and discomfort of intense physical conditioning with inspiration and pride. We support and reinforce each other in accepting these kinds of temporary discomforts. But when it comes to accepting the temporary mental discomfort that may happen as we go within ourselves to meditate we are a nation of wimps. Very few people are willing to do it. Yet this is the activity with the greatest potential for giving us awesome, fulfilling lives.

PUTTING IT ALL TOGETHER - SUMMARY OF THE UNIVERSAL PATH

Here is a schematic that takes all the ideas and terms you have read about so far and shows them in a step by step, linear progression. Of course reality is not linear – it is multi-dimensional and each individual will have their way of approaching the universal path. But this schematic can help your rational brain understand how it works. The keywords that were explained above are in **bold**.

Step One: You start out looking for some combination of happiness, success and pleasure in the external world. Through your ignorance you accumulate a load of **samskaras** that cause you various forms of suffering. Ouch!

Step Two: Eventually **vairagya** and disillusionment hits. You may go to some very low points. If you are wise this motivates you to research what will really work to set you free from suffering. (Otherwise you may spend years, decades or lifetimes cycling through various forms of drama, karma and astral distractions[38] until the **vairagya** is strong enough to make you get serious about true freedom)

Step Three: If you are fortunate enough to get good guidance and mentorship you would learn more about the true art of living, and start practicing your Dharma (fulfilling life path). This would include your commitments to:

• Stop doing any activities that harm others or yourself
• Engage in activities that benefit and bless others and yourself
• Internal meditation practices to purify your mind

Step Four: As you meditate regularly on your breath and the sensations in your body it really sinks in that everything about your life and the world is in **annicha** constant change and flux. This deepens your resolve to connect with the real source of love, peace and fulfillment within yourself. As you practice you gradually learn how to dial back your reactions that take you into craving and aversion. You get better at maintaining **equanimity** of mind.

Step Five: Following through on these commitments gradually brings purification to your deep mind. It becomes easier to enjoy your calm center and you become more unfreakable. You find yourself enjoying more joyful moments and inspired thoughts.

Step Six: If your desire for freedom and fulfillment is strong enough and you get the needed support the veil of ignorance parts

[38] I am using the term "astral distractions" to refer to experiences of the astral plane – a realm of rarified higher mind. The experiences of angels and demons, astral travel, most spirit guide communication, metaphysics and the like come from this level. While useful and fascinating the astral plane is still dualistic and part of *anachur* – impermanence. Therefore it is not possible to find true inner peace on this level and it can be a more refined source of "weapons of mass distraction" to the serious seeker.

more and more. You identify less with the false, small self and increasingly know yourself to be the true, divine Self. Your life changes in many small and large ways and you more easily and frequently bring blessings to others you are in contact with.

Outcome: Thus you experiencing increasing degrees of **enlightenment** and become a light unto the world. You are no longer part of the problem and are now a positive change agent. This will happen whether you are leading a worldwide movement or taking it easy in a retirement home. Regardless of what actions you are doing your being radiates love and wisdom.

OK, SO HOW DO I SIGN UP?

The practices that follow in this section will help you. Each is a form of inner focus, and are simple, practical and proven to work. Some will work for you better than others. Part of your research is to take each practice for a test drive by practicing it and experiencing the benefits for yourself.

There are seven chapters that follow, each detailing an aspect of practice. **In reality these are not separate practices. They are all aspects of the same universal path.** I have presented them in separate chapters to make it easier to develop your practice one step at a time in small, bite-sized chunks.

There is no way to fail at these practices unless you simply don't do them. Whether or not you actually do them is a measure of how much vairagya you have been through! When you know that you really want deep peace, love and calmness of mind, and that you are not going to find it outside it is not so hard to get motivated to start putting your attention where you actually will find it.

There is also an 8 week planner to systematically take you through a sequence of practices that you will find in *Chapter 8, Practice Plan.* Using this is an organized, guided way to get on your universal path of dharma one simple step at a time.

I recommend that you read this current chapter a few times, as there is a lot here. Contemplate what comes up for you as you consider these ideas. Remember, whatever thoughts and feelings come up for you are part of your purification process. Get excited about this, at least as much as an athlete training for the next big event, or a scientist on the verge of her greatest discovery.

7

How to Do the Practices

Better than knowledge is meditation. But better still
is surrender in love, because there follows immediate peace
-- FROM THE BHAGAVAD GITA

What are some things you do every day?

Brush your teeth? Eat? Wash up? Walk your dog? Most of us have rituals like these that we do every day without fail. We just know that we must do these things to survive, or at least not smell bad.

Yet very few people are committed to daily practices that could preserve their peace of mind and help them fulfill the greater promise of their life. Most say they are too busy, or are just basically freaked out by the prospect of slowing down enough to go within, or as my daughter so eloquently says "look at their s--t".

In this Section you will learn remarkably powerful inner practices that you can really do, regardless of your previous beliefs about how "good" a meditator you are. Making a commitment to do inner practices will make a huge difference in your quality and enjoyment of life, and your health. Even an initial commitment of 5 - 10 minutes of practice, twice a day is a great start, and can change your life. These are food for your soul, and will support you in transforming your stress into inner peace.

To make it easy as pie for you to learn these practices, I have made videos of me leading you in practicing most of them. I have also made printable summary sheets to guide you through each practice. You can access those resources for free by going to my website www.drstarwynn.com and registering as a free member. Once you do that you can print out the instructions sheets and watch these videos as much as you want until you have internalized the practices.

ABOUT THE PRACTICES

When you look at the list of practices in this section it may seem that there are a lot of them and it may look intimidating. Please know that all of these are very simple and only a few of them require you sitting down to do them. Some of them are about building your awareness as you are going about your day to day living.

In truth all the techniques you will learn in this section are aspects of one practice. These are all aspects of the Universal Path written about in *Chapter 6*. The Universal Path is common to all useful spiritual paths, and the inner truth behind the major religions.[39] It is about being a conscious human being who is true to who you really are and committed to love and service. It is a useful teaching tool to "chunk the universal path down" into different techniques to practice when you are starting out. Eventually all of these will come together into one unified practice that fills your life. You probably won't be blissful all the time and you will still deal with many of the same things you do now. The difference will be that you will learn to stay connected with your inner peaceful essence through it all. That's a big deal.

---

[39] All the major religions started with one or more inspired teachers who were experiencing and teaching the universal path. After the death of these original teachers religions tend to become encumbered with rites, rituals and dogmas that replace the purity and power of the universal path.

Learning to tune into your calm center may be somewhat chaotic at first. No problem, this is normal. You just need to persist and you will start feeling moments of peace and calm, like you are just where you would love to be. Then it is likely you will lose focus on your calm center and it may feel hard to find it again. Then you will tune into inner calm again. This is the process of gaining mastery. You just need to keep on keeping on. Hold your clear intent that you really want to live in love and conscious presence. Line up the power of your desire with the power of your longing for true connection. I guarantee you that if you persist in this your calm center will become more and more present to you. The greatest gift is when your calm center becomes as real, or even more real to you than your thoughts and the outside world.

Although these practices are simple, they can be extraordinarily powerful. Any of them can rapidly shift you into feeling grounded and at peace. I consider them to be 5D, or fifth dimensional practices. What that means is that the purpose is not to change you, fix you or even "heal" you in the traditional sense. These practices simply refocus you into the part of yourself that is already whole and loving. That is your true Self. This is the part of you that has never been wounded or traumatized, and is always available to you.[40]

Any practice or exercise can be done with various degrees of benefit. Here are ways you can gain the most benefit from working with all the practices in this section:

1. *Don't try to get there – you are already there*

Our egos usually fight to maintain its illusion of separation from our spiritual source. Before starting to go within the ego often fights to keep you from doing it. It will try to convince you with some of these stories: "it is too hard", "I just can't meditate", "I'm too busy", "I need to be ironing my clothes now"[41] and the like.

---

[40] See Chapter 16 for more about fifth dimensional healing.

[41] Even if you don't own an iron.

Now here's something interesting. Once you start enjoying and loving your inner practice the ego may change its tactics. It may start telling you "yes, it's great to do this practice – atta boy! Let's try hard now to reach the goal of inner peace."

This is an even more devious weapon of mass distraction. In reality, there is nowhere to go, nothing to strive for. Enter your practice time with the belief that you are already everything you could want.

Here's a more earthly analogy. Let's say that you have a $100,000 luxury car sitting in front of your house that belongs to you. It is dirty due to a rainstorm. As you start washing it, you don't need to think "Oh God, please give me a nice car!". You already HAVE the car. It just takes a little maintenance to be able to fully enjoy it. That is how I see meditation practice.

2. *Tap into the power of intention*

Intention is the same power that created the Universe. To get more of a flavor of why that is, read Wayne Dyer's book *The Power of Intention.* [42] You can tap into that awesome power simply by calling upon it. As you start any practice say something like this: "It is my intention, as the conscious being that I am, to fully experience the power and virtue of this practice." You can substitute other terms for "conscious being" such as "master being", "spirit being" or whatever inspires you. Once you take that second to set your intention put yourself fully into the practice, even if it is for just a few minutes.

Another powerful intention is to connect with your spiritual source, or higher power, as you do the practice (see 4. below)

3. *Love melts all blockages*

Simply do the practices with love. Love for yourself, love for God or Spirit, love for all the people in your life. Why them? Simple. The more you are grounded in your calm center the more your life

[42] Dyer, Wayne The Power of Intention, Hay House 2004

blesses those around you (or at least annoys them less). You don't even have to try.

Think of the person, animal, place or spiritual being that brings up love the most naturally and easily for you. Allow the feeling of love for that one to touch your heart. Then consciously direct that feeling of love toward yourself and the practice.

4. *Connect with Spirit*

I realize that people reading this book have many different belief systems about spirituality and a higher power. It is not my purpose to introduce any new belief system or change yours, even if you are an atheist. Regardless of your beliefs, if you are reading this I am quite sure you are breathing. As you will read below, breath is spirit.

A powerful way to get your mind and emotions engaged in your practice is to invoke what you feel to be a higher power. Simply do that with whatever higher power or spiritual source you believe in or feel connected with. Humans have felt a direct connection with the numinous, or Divine since ancient times. This works whether you call this numinous quality God, spirit, the Universe, Allah, the Christ, Brahma, Great Spirit, Divine Mother/Father, Tao, nature or a host of other names. This has a number of significant benefits.

First of all, you can't fight fire with fire. The purpose of all of these practices is to help you bring your mind into your calm center. The mind contains and tends to perpetuate pain and trauma programs. Therefore using techniques of the mind such as visualization, positive thinking, chanting mantras or cognitive therapies can be useful, but by definition are limited. The only way to truly heal the mind is to connect it with a power that is bigger than itself.

For example, one of the most successful healing programs in history is Alcoholics Anonymous. There are now over 115,000 groups in the world, and it is one of the only methods that has been proven to help large numbers of alcoholics get and stay sober. Although AA is not affiliated with any religion the founders realized that it is only by acknowledging a higher power that alcoholics could beat their addiction. They understood that for alcoholics no amount of self-discipline or trying to reason with the mind usually accomplishes that.

Turn your practices over to your higher power (or higher Self) as you do them. This is the most effective way to enter into the heart of the practice, and to open and heal your heart.

These practices work in various ways to help you feel more connected, grounded, clearer, stronger and happier. Knowing the truth of your life – freeing yourself to move forward creating a life of passion and purpose.

There is no rush to do these practices, there is no timeline. These are for your life. These are the kinds of things that should have been taught to us in kindergarten, but weren't. As you enter this next stage of your journey of self-discovery and fulfillment, put aside everything that you think you know. Put aside past disappointments and beliefs about what truth is or what healing is or isn't. Come with curiosity, come with eagerness if you can and partake of these practices. I have extensively worked with every single one of them until I have tasted the fruits of the practice. You can also.

If you are inspired to dive into the practices, go to the next chapter now. If you still feel shaky or uncertain about meditating reassure yourself with these truths:

1. Don't even think about trying to do the practices perfectly. If you do them at all that is approaching perfection.

2. It's normal to feel resistance, noisy mind chatter, uncertainty, self-doubt or distraction at times as you start to focus within yourself. Don't think these experiences are "bad" or prove that you are a dummy at meditating. The opposite is true.

3. Know that all people who you have admired as masters of anything went through lots of the same stuff you are on their way to getting to where they are now. The biggest difference between a

master and less accomplished people is that they persevered and did not give up. They connected with a strong desire within themselves and were not willing to live without having what they desired.

Don't waste time struggling with resistance and self-judgment. When your Witness consciousness becomes aware that you have lost focus simply bring your attention back to the steps of the practice. That's it – simple. Know that if your mind wanders a million times and you bring it back within a million times you are doing it right. It will get easier.

AN IMPORTANT NOTE FOR PEOPLE WHO THINK THEY JUST CAN'T MEDITATE (and so may not even try)

So many people have told me that they have tried to meditate, but just could not do it because their minds were too wild and wooly. Please allow me to clear up this misunderstanding for you.

Thinking you just can't meditate comes from the false belief that people who can meditate just close their eyes, turn off their minds and go into deep inner bliss. Perhaps a tiny minority of people can do that easily. Most of us, however, experience much of the same noisy mind as you do. I understand that it may not feel good at first to go within and be with that. Please understand that the act of being willing to feel your own discomfort, while breathing consciously IS part of the practice of meditation.

I'm not saying that meditation needs to be painful and uncomfortable. Once you get into it is one of the most pleasurable experiences you could have. Just like working out and esthetics you may need to go through some temporary discomfort as you start to go within and feel some of your own resistance. I will do my best to inspire you to WANT to do that as you read this section.

8

8 WEEK
PRACTICE PLAN

*The degree of freedom from unwanted thoughts and
the degree of concentration on a single thought
are the measures to gauge spiritual progress.*
-- RAMANA MAHARSHI

All the practices offered in this Section are parts of one activity, the process of awakening to the love and consciousness of your true Self through your personal, body-felt experience. Each chapter in this Section offers a simple practice that has been proven to support this process.

If you would like to "cut to the chase" and go right away to the practice that will have the deepest effect on purifying your mind and taking you into your calm center, it would be the conscious breathwork practices presented in Chapter 12.

You may benefit more, however if you progress through the different aspects of practice in a step-by-step progression. In this chapter I offer an eight week plan to launch new meditators on their inner journey. This plan could also help experienced meditators get re-invigorated and re-inspired. Many of us who have meditated for years or decades have settled into a limited plateau in our experience of meditation. This often happens because meditation has become a routine. We may be focusing on the aspect of meditation that comes most easily to us, and avoiding the areas of personal development that are more challenging.

For example, some people drawn to meditation have well-developed intuitive abilities, and may be able to sense the presence of subtle energies, soul communication and spiritual guides. As a result they tend to meditate by "tuning in" to these and feeling the higher level energies they bring. While this can be a wonderful experience, it alone will not purify the mind and remove the deep core of suffering. Other people who are more mentally based may enjoy guided meditation recordings or videos, or benefit from repeating affirmations and mantras. They may be inspired by reading inspirational or metaphysical books and attending workshops. Again, while these activities can be beneficial on many levels in themselves they also will not liberate you from the root of pain and separation.

The **8 week practice plan** that follows will support you in systematically developing your mental, emotional and spiritual faculties in a more balanced fashion. This will help you clear any roadblocks that could prevent you from receiving the full benefits of meditation. Feel free to experiment with this sequence of practices. Explore within the laboratory of your own body and consciousness to find how meditation really works for you.

HOW TO DO THE 8 WEEK PLAN

1. Make a commitment

There are amazing, unlimited benefits of having a regular meditation practice. It is completely up to you how much of those benefits you will enjoy. You get those benefits by making a firm commitment to prioritize your meditation practice. You can start to gain these benefits even if your initial commitment is for a short as 5 minutes, twice a day.

Choose a block of time each day for your practice and do your best to stick to it. No matter how busy and involved your life is you CAN do this if you really want to. Remember the old saying – "If you give a task to a very busy person she is more likely to get it done than someone with lots of time on her hands". This is true because most busy, effective people have learned how to optimize and budget their time, at least to some extent.

Whether or not you actually follow through with your meditation practice is a measure of how much vairagya you have experienced (see Chapter 6 for explanation of vairagya, the gripping experience of disillusionment that most strongly propels us to go within ourselves). When you get to a point in your life of deeply feeling that you are NOT going to find love and satisfaction outside of yourself is when you will be motivated to make the effort to meditate consistently.

It is best to do your practices during the same times each day. Doing that will stabilize your mind and body and create a healthy meditation habit. It will be best if you choose two periods of time each day, such as 15 minutes in the morning and 15 minutes in the evening. If you can't do that right away at least choose one regular daily time slot.

Here is how you get really serious about the commitment – list your daily meditation time(s) in the same planner you use for your daily work and activities. This could be a schedule book or on-line calendar from Google, Yahoo or others. You probably already take your work scheduling commitments very seriously because they pay your bills and put food on your table. When you list your meditation time on your calendar you are recognizing that it is just as vital for your life!

2. Journal

Start a fresh notebook for journaling your experiences and insights as you progress through the 8 week plan and beyond. This is a vital part of your mindfulness practice, the basis of becoming more conscious.

3. Doing it

For each step of the plan listed below, read the recommended chapter of this book and work through the processes and practices in it. Repeat the same practices each day for the recommended number of days, intending to go deeper into your experience. Use your journal to record a few notes about what you are experiencing, or to write down any questions that arise. It is likely you will be able to answer your own questions as you progress in the plan. If not you can seek the support of others.

4. Set a timer

I recommend that you find a timer app on your smartphone, or get a simple, dumb timer used for cooking or other purposes (but not one that you can hear ticking). For each meditation period set the timer for the length of time you have committed to, and practice at least until your hear the timer chime go off at the end of the period. This is important because it prevents your mind from thinking and worrying about whether your meditation time is over or not, or creating excuses to cut it short. Using a timer helps you let go of all that so you can relax and focus on meditating.

If you use a smart phone timer it is essential that you turn off all other ring tones for phone calls or text messages during your practice time. Again, this is a demonstration of your clear intention to prioritize your meditation during your practice time. The odds of your loved ones dying or the world ending during your meditation time are extremely remote!

5. Persevere

Don't expect it to be easy. Don't expect it to always feel good. Don't expect it to be feel bad. Don't expect anything! All that matters is that you do the meditation technique patiently and persistently. Resolve to stay with your practice until your timer sounds.

6. Practice equanimity

As described in Chapter 6 equanimity of mind is a major key to meditation. Train yourself to be unattached to either pleasant or unpleasant sensations that come up as you practice. It is our reactions to pleasant or unpleasant sensations that create *samskaras* and increase our core suffering. Follow the KISS formula (Keep it Simple, Sadhu![43]). Simply do the techniques as explained and have no attachment to what it looks or feels like. KNOW that you are having the perfect experience for you. Truly, the only way you can fail is if you don't do the practices at all.

7. Have an accountability partner

I suggest that you find someone with whom you can work through this practice plan, so you can support each other and share about your experiences. Such a person could be called an "accountability partner". You make an agreement to check in periodically with each other to see how each of you are doing and how you are keeping up your commitment to do your inner work. You could also work with a professional therapist or coach for this purpose. For many people just knowing that you will be checking in with your accountability partner helps bolster personal motivation to keep moving forward and not make excuses to yourself for procrastinating on doing your practices.

[43] Sadhu is a Sanskrit word referring to people who are monks or otherwise dedicated to spiritual practice. I am using it here humorously, not to indicate that you need to live like a monk to enjoy meditation. Those of us who are meditating while living complex lives full of passions, relationships and commitments could be referred to as the "sadhus of the West". We are blazing new pathways quite different than the traditional model of committed spirituality from Indian or Western monastic traditions.

Before starting on this program, I suggest that you read *Chapter 6: The Universal Path* if you have not already done so. This will help you understand the bigger picture of the benefits of these practices. You may want to come back and re-read that chapter periodically as you progress with your program. As you have more experiences of meditation you will understand the Universal Path in deeper ways.

Know that the suggested practice plan that follows is a guideline only. What is of greatest importance is you learning to follow your own inner guidance. Feel free to modify or adapt this plan in a way that works best for you. You may want to linger on any of the following steps for more than one week, or skip some parts and come back to them later. Remember, you are a sovereign being. While instructions and guidelines are valuable and supportive at times YOU are the ultimate authority on what it takes to fulfill your life.

A Note about Procrastination

&

Are you motivated to follow this practice plan but find yourself procrastinating as you start on it? Rather than allowing this tendency to control you, or berating yourself for being "bad" at meditating use this as an exercise in consciousness. Set your intention to connect with and heal the procrastinating part of you. Invoke this part by saying something like "I now choose to connect with the procrastinating part of me." Intend to bring the light of your true Self into that area and imagine light filling it.

Make a powerful statement such as "I now choose to take charge of my meditation and inner work and do what my soul (higher self) is leading me to do".

THE EIGHT WEEK PLAN

WEEK ONE

First 3 days of the week:

- Read: *Chapter 9 – Body Energy Hook Up*
- Practice: **9-1 - Body Energy Hook up**. Use it as much as you can throughout your daily routines.

Last 4 days of the week:

- Read *Chapter 10 – Mindfulness*
- Practice: **10.1 - Mindfulness in daily life**
- Continue with Body Energy Hook Up

WEEK TWO

- Read: Complete reading *Chapter 10 – Mindfulness*
- Practice: Continue with **10-1 - Mindfulness in daily life**.
- Continue with this awareness throughout the rest of the program. This is not just a practice, it is a new way of living!
- Also do: **10-2 - Mindfulness of the sensations in your body**
- Do practice 10-2 daily for at least one week

WEEK THREE

- Read: *Chapter 11 – Clearing Your Inner Space*, section on Energy Tapping
- Practice: **11-1 - Instructions for using energy tapping**
- Familiarize yourself with the basic procedure. Try using it any time you feel stressed, overwhelmed or afraid. You can

also use it for self-care and uplifting your consciousness when you are feeling good.

- Continue with **10-1 - Mindfulness in daily life**. This is not just a practice, it is a new way of living!

WEEK FOUR

- Continue to work with: *Chapter 11 – Clearing Your Inner Space*
- Practices: **11-1 - Instructions for using energy tapping**
- Continue to experiment with energy tapping.
- Practice: **11-2 - Immediate Release Technique (IRT)**
- Read this section and practice this simple technique a few times until you are comfortable with it.
- Practice: **- 11-3 - Combining energy tapping with IRT**

Try using these methods any time you feel stressed, overwhelmed or afraid. You can also use them for self-care when you are feeling good.

If you have been recently been experiencing significant pain or stress, continue focusing on these Week Four practices and mindfulness for two - three weeks before going onto the next practices.

If stress is not a significant issue for you now it is still very valuable to have these practices in your self-care "tool-belt". Practice them enough to get familiar with them, and then use them to clear your inner space the next time you find yourself in challenging times.

WEEK FIVE

If you have been following this program over the last month it is likely that you are progressing in your ability to keep your mind in the Now moment and manage your own stress. It doesn't matter how much progress you think you have made. Just making the effort to do these simple practices makes you successful, regardless of how good you are feeling right now. Remember, craving "feeling good" is another way to create samskaras!

- Start reading: *Chapter 12 – Reclaiming Your Calm Center*
- Practice: **12-1 - 7-7-7 Breathing**

Organize and plan your time so you will do this practice twice a day for at least 5 minutes each time. This is a good time to start bringing this element of healthy self-discipline into your inner life. If you encounter resistance to making this commitment do not judge yourself for that. Bring your resistance into consciousness by examining it and writing about it in your journal. Find out what works for you for creating commitment in yourself to doing your regular daily practice.

Continue with **10-1 - Mindfulness in daily life**. Challenge yourself to increase the number of moments you are mindful of the Now moment in your everyday life. Keep energy tapping and IRT in your self-care toolbelt. These don't need to be regular practices, just use them as needed when you feel stressed or challenged.

WEEK SIX

- Continue reading: *Chapter 12 – Reclaiming Your Calm Center*
- Practice: **12-2 - Mindfulness of Breath.** This includes practices **12-2-A** and **12-2-B.**
- Make sure you read the section in that chapter *"Dealing with resistance or reaction"*. Be aware if you are experiencing any of this, and reach out for support if that is the case.

WEEKS SIX to SEVEN

- Continue reading: *Chapter 12 – Reclaiming Your Calm Center*
- Practice: **12-3 - Anapana Meditation.**

This practice is the most important one in this book. This is the fundamental consciousness-opening and self-healing practice personally practiced and taught by the Buddha, one of our greatest world teachers of enlightenment. It is simple enough for anyone to do. This is a practice you can do for the rest of your life with unlimited benefits and blessings.

You can start with practice times as short as 10 minutes at a time. Gradually increase your practice times as you can. Doing Anapana for 30 – 60 minutes at a time, twice a day will transform your life in a very positive way.

Continue focusing on anapana practice in this practice plan for two weeks. Use the other practices learned in previous weeks as needed. I hope you never stop!

As you commit to a regular practice of anapana stuff may come up because it is purifying your consciousness.

On Week 7 you can also work with **Practice 12-4 - Mindfulness of your calm center** a few times to help you in tuning into your calm center.

WEEK EIGHT

By this time you can be enjoying a regular sitting practice of anapana, and spending more moments being mindful in the Now moment as you go through your daily activities. Doing these activities has the effect of shifting your whole life into an experience of presence – being conscious in the Now moment throughout all of your experiences. In other words you will become more grounded in the truth of your life and who you really are. This is the #1 key to enjoying and fulfilling the great potential of your precious life.

Most people's experiences are full of fears, biases, avoidances and acting out of old, limiting patterns. All of this takes their awareness out of the Now moment much of the time. Being that way seems to be the norm, so as you live more in the Now moment the way you relate to others may change. On one hand it is likely you will be more loving and attentive toward people and animals you meet. On the other hand some of your relationships may shift. You may not want to spend much time anymore around people invested into negativity and complaining. You could be drawn to be with others who are committed to being loving and positive, and embodying their higher light. Trust these impulses because the company you keep has a strong effect on your own state of mind.

In this week you can integrate the Unified Field meditation into your practice, if you have not already done so. Becoming conscious of the Unified Field starts out as a practice you need to sit down and do. If you persist it will eventually become a part of your overall state of consciousness.

- Read Chapter 14 – Unified Field Meditation
- **Practice 14-1 - Unified Field Meditation**

During my practice time I start by quickly going through the steps of the Unified Field meditation, and setting my intention to stay Unified throughout my day. Then I sit down to do Anapana and Vipassana meditation[44].

If you choose to try this for yourself, know that you don't need to keep thinking about the Unified Field as you do anapana, just trust that you are Unified without any further mental energy needed to reinforce that.

AFTER YOU COMPLETE THE 8 WEEK PLAN

Congratulations!

If you have worked through the steps of this plan you have demonstrated to yourself that you are very motivated and sincere about healing yourself and fulfilling your life purpose. Now you have the rest of your life to enjoy and share who you are.

---

[44] Vipassana meditation cannot be adequately taught in a book. See information about it in the Resources section in the end of this book.

As stated earlier, all the practices presented in this section are really aspects of one unified practice, and that is living a conscious, fulfilling life internally connected with your spiritual source. As you experience the truth behind all the practices in this section they will flow together and create your version of the universal path.

My ongoing daily practices include Anapana, Vipassana, working with decrees and words of power and aligning with my true Self. Now that you have worked through the 8 week plan you probably have a sense of what practices work best for you. It is my sincere desire that you continue making inner practice a priority for the rest of your life, adapting it to your needs and inspirations.

It is valuable to create support systems for your meditation practice and living your awakened life. Find people or groups of people you can connect with regularly who are prioritizing that as well. If there is no group in your area you resonate with consider starting your own group. That is a great service and will further your own growth as your light becomes a support for others.

Please see *Chapter 17* and Appendix 2, the Resources section for ideas and links that can help you create your support system and be part of spiritual community.

For those who want to go deeper in their process of self-healing and enlightenment I suggest that you attend one or more 10 day silent Vipassana retreats. Information on these is in the Resource section at the end of the book.

9

Body Energy Hook Up

Spiritual 'exercise' keeps your mind in shape the way
physical exercise keeps your body in shape.
-- MARIANNE WILLIAMSON

How would you like to learn a practice that is so simple that a toddler could do it, and has the power to un-stress and boost you whenever you want? That is what the Body Energy Hook Up is. I have put it first in the practice section so you can have a gratifying practical experience right away.

Practice 9.1 - Body Energy Hook Up

Touch the tip of your tongue to the roof of your mouth, right behind your two front teeth. To find the right location, put the tip of your tongue on the back of your two front teeth. Then move it slightly back (toward the back of your mouth). The tip of your tongue should still be lightly touching the roof of your mouth, but about ¼ inch back from the front teeth. Most people have a ridge on the roof of their mouth just behind that spot.

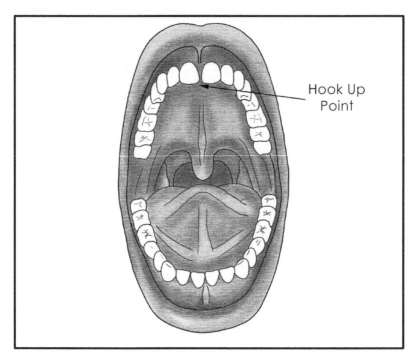

Hook Up
Point

Hook Up spot in mouth

That's it.

Here's an amazing fact. When your tongue is in this position it is very difficult to feel anxiety or stress! Those feelings are usually associated with a sense of unsafety and disconnection. The simple act of keeping your tongue on the roof of your mouth provides a gentle but immediate feeling of inner connection.

It gets even better.

As you probably know the art of acupuncture is based on adjusting the flow of Qi, or vital energy, in the body. Qi flows through defined energy channels called meridians. Meridians are classified as being *Yin* or *Yang*. According to Traditional Chinese Medicine *Yin* energy is nurturing, cooling, receptive, watery and calming. It is considered to be the feminine energy of your body. *Yang* energy is energizing, warming, penetrating, fiery and activating. It is considered to be the male energy of the body.

Meridians act a lot like rivers and streams. Some meridians are like streams running into a bigger river. Two of the biggest major rivers of energy in the body are the Conception Vessel, which runs up the front midline of the body, and the Governing Vessel, which runs up the back midline of the body. Each of the major organs flows its energy through one or more major meridians. Each of these major meridians in the body flow into either the Conception or Governing Vessel, so those are powerful streams of Qi. This is similar to the way smaller streams and tributaries flow into a major river. The original Chinese names for these major meridans are *Du Mai for* Governing Vessel and *Ren Mai* for Conception Vessel.

The Conception Vessel starts in the perineum between the legs and runs up the front midline of the body. It terminates in the mouth. The Governing Vessel starts below the tailbone and runs up the spine, goes over the midline of the head and also ends in the mouth. Thus all the major energy streams of the body's organs end up in the mouth directly or indirectly. Now here's the best part – when you do the Body Energy Hook Up you are literally switching on a circuit breaker in your mouth that connects and balances ALL your body energies. Way cool, eh?

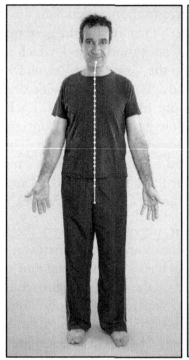 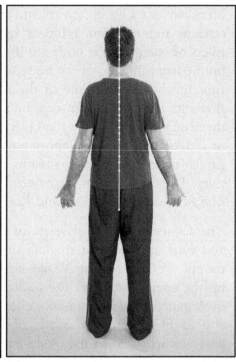

Conception Vessel (Ren Mai) Governing Vessel (Du Mai)

The whole art of acupuncture and Chinese medicine is based on balancing *Yin* and *Yang*. You can give yourself an immediate *Yin - Yang* balancing by doing the Body Energy Hook Up.

Qi has an electrical aspect. When I do the Body Energy Hook Up I feel a subtle electrical connection on the tip of my tongue. I know that it's electrical because as a child I experimented with putting my tongue across the terminals of electrical batteries, feeling the zap of current. This reminds me a little of that, but of course much gentler and smoother.

Take it for a test drive. Try to keep your tongue in that position more of the time whenever you need extra energy, focus or concentration. Use it to enhance relaxation, stress reduction or bolster you when you need to face a challenging situation. Experiment with keeping your tongue there whenever you meditate, pray or do your creative thing. There is no limit to the benefits of this instant balancer.

You will be advised to combine the Body Energy Hook Up with the practices you will learn in the rest of the chapters in this section.

10

Mindfulness

*Whatever arises in the mind is accompanied
by a sensation in the body*
-- BUDDHA

Mindfulness practices are all the rage these days - because they work. Mindfulness is keeping your attention in present time as much as possible, and being a witness to your moment by moment experiences.

The most important experiences to be mindful of are the sensations within your body. Remember, your body is always truthful and is always in the now moment. That is rarely true of our minds and emotions. **It is your body that is your personal gateway to healing and enlightenment.**

Being mindful of the actual experience of being alive is very different than being aware of your thoughts, beliefs, judgments and fears about it. These are collectively called your "stories", and are not very helpful in the healing process. Yet most people get stuck dwelling on their stories much of the time instead of directly experiencing their life.

Human beings are multi-dimensional. We live and experience on many levels. In reality we are the true Self that is an expression of our spiritual source and all life. Yet our human minds and personalities have many facets are often in conflict with each other.

Psychologists have long recognized that we are not just one unified personality. All of us have many "parts" that make up who we are. Have you ever noticed that you may act one way with your best friend, another way with your child and another way with your boss? One part of me is a goofy jokester, another is a confident public speaker, another part is an insecure abandoned child, one part can be a sensual man and another part is a meditative spiritual monk.

These different parts of us are called *subpersonalities*. This has been written about by psychologists Jung, Freud and James. Having different subpersonalities is a normal part of human nature. These are aspects of yourself that each have a mind and a personality of its own. It's like having several different mini-me's roaming around in your consciousness. To the extent we are psychologically healthy we flow in and out of the expressions of our subpersonalities while staying in touch with our real core. Another way of saying this is that we stay grounded in our calm center while experiencing all the shifting sands (or hurricane winds) of our life.

Traumatized people often have a hard time staying in touch with their core. Their subpersonalities take on stronger lives of their own, and can become more split off from each other. Psychiatrists often diagnose this as *dissociative identity disorder* (DID), formerly called multiple personality disorder.

People suffering with DID are often put on medications to try to control their symptoms. It is much more helpful for them to receive support and training in the skills needed to reclaim their core. Practicing mindfulness has been proven to be an important part of therapy for people with DID and PTSD.

The most powerful way to reclaim your calm center is to get in touch with your true Self through conscious breath. From that place be mindful of the different parts of your personality dancing in and out of your awareness. There are many psychological systems for helping people feel more integration among their subpersonalities. One notable example is IFS, or Internal Family Systems developed by Richard Schwartz[45].

You know you are practicing mindfulness when someone does something to hurt your feelings and instead of instantly reacting you say to yourself "Interesting - there I am feeling hurt and wanting to defend myself and lash out". That part of yourself that is observing your emotional reactions is your pure consciousness and calm center and congratulations, you are getting to know it.

A word of common sense: practicing mindfulness does not mean that you will detach from your emotions and deny them. There is nothing wrong with anger, grief, sadness, elation or feeling down sometimes. These are our real human feelings. So allow yourself to feel the full richness and textures of your emotions. The key is staying attuned to your core, the Self, through it all.

If you have been out of touch with your feelings, or have felt emotionally numb, practicing mindfulness may help you to feel your emotions more. This is because you will be less likely to judge and reject yourself for feeling them. If you feel that you have been too ruled by your emotions it is also important to move out of self-judgment. Practicing mindfulness can help you learn to be in mastery of your feelings by staying grounded and accepting yourself and all your experiences.

As you start to practice mindfulness it is good to do it in a quiet place where you can concentrate. As you train yourself to be mindful you will be able to do it anywhere, including loud, busy places. In fact those are great places to practice mindfulness.

45 https://www.selfleadership.org/

MINDFULNESS IN DAILY LIFE

The most valuable form of mindfulness is that which you practice throughout all the experiences of your life. There is a part of your awareness that is often called the Witness. This is pure consciousness that observes all of your experiences. The Witness part of you has no judgments or biases, it simply experiences. This part of you is the same whether you are feeling joy or feeling upset or hurt. This Witness is the conscious Self within you, and it is always available.

Try to extend your ability to be mindful into more and more parts of your life. If you are the competitive type see it as a challenge and compete with yourself to see how much you can increase your score of staying mindful. If you are a more heart centered person be motivated by the increased love you can feel when you are truly present in the Now moment.

A core teaching of the Buddha is vital to revisit here. As mentioned in Chapter 6 he taught that the root cause of our deepest suffering is our **reactions** to the sensations of life[46]. We react by craving pleasant sensations and having aversion to unpleasant sensations. Remember this as you practice mindfulness. As you move into these next practices intend to become aware of your "craving" and "aversion" reactions. When you see yourself reacting to anything put your tongue on the roof of your mouth and practice conscious, deeper breathing. What this does is substitute conscious awareness for unconscious reactions. This is unlikely to take away all your reactions right away. But you will certainly be well on your path of self-healing and awakening.

Practice 10-1: Mindfulness in Daily Life

This practice is all about becoming more conscious of your experiences in the moment using the tool of the Body Energy Hook Up, as taught in *Chapter 9*. Simply practice that as much as

[46] These reactions are what creates Samskaras, the painful and limiting conditioning of our subconscious mind that is the root of human suffering

you can throughout your day, while breathing deeply as much as you can. Whenever you do these two things you will tend to feel more connected to yourself. They also make it easier to keep your attention in the now moment.

From this place of increased connectedness and presence see the experiences of your life with fresh eyes. This is mindfulness. Practice this when:

- You wake up in the morning

- You are doing any habitual action, like eating, getting ready for your day, meeting a partner or friend, working, driving, walking, going to the bathroom, or getting ready to sleep.

- You are facing any stressful situation that in the past made you react in uncomfortable ways. Being mindful does not mean that won't experience any stress. It can help you to feel more grounded in yourself, thereby putting you more in control of your reactions.

- You are doing any kind of prayer, meditation or the like.

You will get a lot more value from this exercise if you record your experiences and insights in a journal regularly. When you look back and read your journal entries after a few weeks it is likely you will have some valuable insights about yourself.

Three areas of life that provide you wonderful opportunities to practice mindfulness are relationships, finances and health issues. Here are a few guidelines for being mindful in each of these:

1. Intimate Relationships

Intimate relationships usually take us through experiences ranging from pure, selfless loving to painful, angry reactions. Some of our feelings and actions in relationships are relatively conscious, meaning that we choose them. Other experiences seem to explode out of deep, hidden parts of our psyche. Most of our negative reactions in relationships actually have little to nothing to do with our present partner. They arise when a triggering experience with your partner reminds the amygdala-hippocampus circuit of our brain of a past hurt. In this sense they are a form of low-grade PTSD[47].

The next time you are with your partner, a boss or anyone else you have had difficult times with, intend to practice mindfulness. By keeping your tongue on the roof of your mouth and breathing consciously you will develop more of your Witness consciousness. Your Witness will help you observe yourself reacting, or wanting to react. When you can "see" yourself doing that you move more into choice about whether you express it or not.

2. Finances

Most of us are psychologically wired with set beliefs and reactions about money that keep us limited in the amount of it we have. This is what T. Harv Eker calls your *"money set point"*[48]. This is a big one! Depending on your upbringing and life experiences you may have any of these habitual thoughts about money:

- Ease and abundance
- Scarcity, fear, worry
- A never-ending quest to accumulate more of it
- Guilt or obligation that compels you to keep losing it or giving it away
- Disliking it and having a minimum of it around
- Hoarding it

Practice money mindfulness by allowing your Witness consciousness to observe your thoughts and feelings as you do financial transactions. Notice where your attention is drawn to in your body. Do the Body Energy Hook Up and breathe into this body part. If you wish to change your limiting beliefs about money you can combine doing this with Energy Tapping and words of power (Chapter 11, Appendix 3).

[47] See Chapter 2 for explanation of how the brain works in regards to triggering experiences
[48] Eker, T. Harv, The Millionaire Mind, Harper Business, 2005

3. Health

Mindfulness can literally shift your patterns of pain and disease simply by applying consciousness to imbalanced parts of your body. Are you in pain, feel sick to your stomach, or have no energy? Is your body inflamed or do you have tumors in it? In any case step back from fear or judgement about your body and practice mindfulness.

Tune into the part of your body manifesting the symptom, breathe into it, do the tongue hookup and observe. Radiate your pure love and support to that part without any urge to fix or change it. Be attentive to whatever feelings, images or thoughts arise as your become mindful of the hurting parts of your body/mind. The messages you may receive could be keys to what is required to resolve the pain or disease at its root.

Mindfulness meditation has been demonstrated to significantly reduce chronic pain and the symptoms of diseases in many clinical studies. See footnote for an example[49].

HEALING YOUR MIND THROUGH YOUR BODY

This vital truth is another key teaching of the Buddha:

Whatever arises in the mind is accompanied by a sensation (in the body)

This is a key discovery. It is very difficult to directly control our minds or reason with our strong emotions. Most of us have tried to do that and found out just how hard that is. It is much easier to focus on physical sensations in our body. Focusing our attention on sensations in our body and our breath are the most valuable forms of meditation. When done with commitment and regularity these are the meditations best able to purify and heal the deep root of pain and suffering and take you into your calm center.

You will have a great opportunity to practice mindfulness the next time you feel mentally agitated or emotionally triggered. Have a

49 Journal of Behavioral Medicine, June 1985, Volume 8, Issue 2, pp 163–190

time out and take a deep breath. Using your mind scan through your body and ask yourself which part is most strongly registering that upset feeling. Once you discover your body area most strongly connected with the feeling put the palm of one hand over that area[50] and focus your attention there. Breathe intentionally into that body area. With simple awareness and curiosity notice what the sensation feels like there. These sensations could include heat, cold, tightness, aching, strong pulsing, or a cloaked or covered up feeling. Of course there could be others.

From this point of awareness relax and feel into this body part. Detach yourself from analysis, judgment or stories about the thoughts or feelings you are having. Just be with the actual sensations in your body. As you stop labelling and resisting them, and simply relax and breathe into the feelings with mindfulness you can experience them in a new way. You are healing yourself with the power of pure awareness. It is even better if you can direct your love into the body part you are focusing on. The Inner Smile practice described in *Chapter 13* will guide you in doing that.

If your disturbing feelings or thoughts are strong and persistent the tapping and eye movement exercises explained in *Chapter 11* are likely to help you rapidly ease and transform them.

Practice 10-2: Mindfulness of the Sensations in your Body

There is aliveness and consciousness in every part of your body. For the purpose of this exercise I will call this the *"soul"* of each body part.[51] In the practice that follows you will be asking the souls of parts of your body to help you feel the energy in those parts. This is a very valuable mindfulness practice. It will go far to help you feel grounded, balanced and in love with your own body.

We will start with progressive relaxation. Put your body in a comfortable position and breathe deeply throughout this exercise. Tighten all the muscles in

---

[50] Putting your hand over a body part draws more healing energy there, and helps you focus your attention there.

[51] This is distinct from the belief of many religions in one single soul.

your feet, hold a moment, then release. Follow with the muscles in both legs. Then tighten, hold and relax the muscles in your pelvic area. Follow with your belly and low back area, then your chest and upper back. Next tighten, hold and relax both shoulders, followed by both arms and hands. Next tighten, hold and relax your neck, followed by all the muscles in your head and face.

Bring your attention back to your feet. Say or think "Dear soul of my feet. I love you and appreciate you. Please help me to consciously feel the life force energy in my feet." Put your full attention on your feet. Imagine you are directing your breath in and out of your feet. Tune into the sensations there. Is there any pain or discomfort? Any good feelings? Can you feel a gentle tingling of energy in your feet? Any sensations of heat or cold or pulsing? If you feel something, anything, that is great. Be with that sensation and breathe into it.

Are there any emotions or memories that come up as you tune into your feet? Feeling those are just as valuable as feeling the energy itself.

If you don't think you can feel anything in your feet try tightening and loosening your feet a few times and bring your attention there again. Try gently stamping them up and down on the floor a few times to stimulate the energy flow. Try declaring "It is my intention to open myself to directly feeling the energy in my body." Do you feel anything in your feet now?

Next tune into the sensation in your legs in the same way. Ask the soul of your legs to help you feel the energy in your legs. Practice feeling the gentle tingle of the energy in your legs, or however you experience it. If anything comes up for you as you tune into your legs, simply be with that experience and breathe into it.

For these other parts of your body, follow the same method.

Tune into your belly – your major power center and feel.

Follow with your Heart/ chest area.

Finish by tuning into the sensations in your head.

Repeat with any other part of your body you choose.

Finish by thanking the souls within your body for being there and supporting you.

You cannot fail at this technique. If you directly feel the energy in each area that is great. You are already aware of your inner body. If it is very hard for you to feel anything, just be aware of how it feels to not feel anything – even if the feeling is frustration. Even if you feel completely numbed out to any kind of feelings just take the time to love yourself being numb. Say to yourself "I love myself feeling numbed out. I feel compassion for what I must have gone through to be this way."

If you start feeling bad or frustrated because it is hard for you to feel the energy in your body, or if you feel discomfort in your body know that this is a form of aversion. As explained above, substitute awareness for aversion and simply be a witness to the sensation you are experiencing.

Don't give up. Journal about your experiences doing this exercise.

11

Clearing Your Inner Space

Knowledge of the self is the mother of all knowledge. So it is incumbent on me to know myself, to know it completely, to know its minutiae, its characteristics, its subtleties, and its very atoms.
-- KHALIL GIBRAN

Most traditional cultures have created mythologies that have been passed down through the generations. Myths are the stories of gods, demons, heroes, animals and ordinary people that exemplify the human experience. The most enduring myths are rich in archetypes. Archetypes are universal core experiences shared by people across many times and cultures. Archetypes include the Warrior, the Mother, the Hero, the Lover, the Betrayer, the Magician, the Divine, the Joker, etc. Myths with archetypal characters are often externalizations of the inner process of self-realization and healing.

One such Greek myth that I read over and over growing up is the Odyssey. This is the story of Odysseus, a king from the island of Ithaca who sailed with a Greek army to fight the Trojan War. After the Greeks were victorious Odysseus and his men sailed toward home through the Mediterranean Sea and went through many adventures and trials. When Odysseus finally returned to his beloved Ithaca after a 20 year absence he found many male suitors living on his land trying to force his wife Penelope to marry one of them.

It was not easy for one man to defeat all these warriors, and Odysseus knew he needed a clever plan to get them out of his home. So he disguised himself as an old beggar to observe the situation. Finally he came up with a plan and was able to slay all the suitors with the help of his son Telemachus and his servant Laertes. Odysseus then reclaimed his rightful place as Penelope's husband and lord of his estate.

This myth is very significant for the message of this book.

Think of your inner calm center, your wellspring of peace and self-love, as your Ithaca, your true home. You may have experienced the illusion of separation from your all-loving source, as so many of us have in the process of "discombobulation". You are now ready to re-join your inner source of love, your Penelope. As you try to bring your mind back within to your calm center you become aware of how many "suitors" have overrun your inner sanctum and commandeered your resources (your body, mind and emotions). These are the repetitive fear and separation thoughts that make up your monkey mind. You could also understand these "suitors" to be the samskaras described in *Chapter 6*.

Clearing your inner space allows you to reclaim and enjoy your calm center as your constant life experience. Unlike Odysseus, this is not about killing your intrusive thoughts and feelings, it is much more of a process of love and integration. It is vital to have a process for clearing your inner space and keeping it clear and pure so you can enjoy your true estate of inner peace and abiding love.

HOW DO I DEAL WITH EMOTIONAL PAIN?

All of us go through periods of painful or troubled feelings. Most of the time we can cope with our down times through our own emotional resilience and the support of friends and family. People who have been through extensive trauma in their lives often have greater struggles with dark times. It is often harder for them to self-sooth and see the light.

Feeling inner pain at times is a universal experience for all humans, yet the way we look at it varies greatly from culture to culture. In our American worldview most doctors and psychiatrists see anxiety and depression as chemical imbalances that require drug therapies for correction. In other cultures people tend to be more stoic and not complain or speak about their pain much. Many traditional cultures have viewed inner pain as due to violations of the rules of society or as demonic influences.

In my view it is far better to see emotional pain as a signal from our inner self that greater self-love and self-awareness is called for. For those who wish to grow in their personal empowerment pain can be understood to be a door of opportunity. It is a call to practice greater self-connection and self-love than we usually take the time for. Since what I just wrote can sound rather theoretical, I will offer my own experience as an example.

I recently attended a three day workshop in Los Angeles, and while I was at that event I made a big commitment to myself to expand my services to more people. I committed to a year-long program teaching me new skills for developing and running workshops for doctors and holistic health professionals.

On my way home to the San Francisco Bay area I started having uncomfortable feelings in my body. By the time I got home it felt like a flu was coming on. Not wanting to go down that path I pulled out all my herbs and supplements for cold and flu and started taking them. I also made a big pot of chicken soup and did lots of mind and body clearing techniques. I hardly ever get sick, and when I have felt similar symptoms in the past I had been able to dispel them in two or three days by using such remedies.

To my dismay the symptoms got worse and worse. I felt very painful body aches around my chest and heart coupled with nausea, coughing and chills. I was unable to work. I couldn't sleep at night and felt the misery of knowing I badly needed restorative sleep but couldn't get much of it. This went on for days. I chugged loads of immune stimulating herbs, had massages, drank soup, received acupuncture and consulted with two spiritual healers. While all these things helped to some extent the flu symptoms did not abate.

After several nights of this ordeal I knew that there was a message from my body that I had not been listening to. I got out of bed at 3 AM, sat in my living room and got past my lethargy enough to take responsibility for greater self-connection. I stopped resisting the painful body aches and put my full attention and love on the pain. I asked "what is your message?" I practiced the simple tapping and EMDR methods described below for 20 minutes while holding my painful body in love and compassion. As I did this the terrible body aches finally started to diminish. For the first time in days I was able to sleep. Within a couple of days my health and vitality started returning.

There are many ways of understanding this experience. Most people in our culture would say that I caught a nasty flu at my conference, and I just needed time for it to run its course, and for my immune system to rally. I heard people talk about how "there's a lot of that going around these days, I know so many people laid up for a week or more". I believe that is only part of the truth.

What has been going around is a lot of anger and fear about what is happening in our country and our planet. Lots of us have experienced the results of the recent Presidential election here in the USA as a major wake-up call to jolt us out of any sense of complacency about our lives. At the conference I attended just before getting sick I stepped up to make a bigger commitment to being part of the solution. By doing that I opened myself to a bigger sphere of energy and consciousness. This came into conflict with some ways I had been hiding behind my fears and self-doubts about my ability to fulfill my purpose. Kind of like the irresistible force meeting the immovable object!

While some of the painful body aches and other symptoms I felt over that week may have been due to my immune system fighting a virus there was something more. There was a doorway of greater empowerment open to me, and I had to rally my courage and determination to know that the power was within me to walk through it. Each time I did my consciousness practices the pain lessened and my sense of clarity increased. I now understand that the bar has been raised on my need for continued self-responsibility and self-connection. The alleged sickness I went through was a form of difficult spiritual purification centered around my heart.

This view that painful experiences are often part of a spiritual transformation is not new to me. As mentioned earlier I taught many seminars on pain management to doctors and acupuncturists over a 25 year period, and treated hundreds of patients with difficult chronic pain conditions. I was able to help lots of them release their pain, even after they had not found relief elsewhere. The key to these positive results were that I was helping these patients recognize and address the emotional roots of their pain. Other doctors and practitioners had focused on changing the signal of pain – through drugs, acupuncture, physical therapy and more. Of course these methods are often effective. Yet they work inconsistently if not combined with emotional healing and clearing.

ENERGY TAPPING

Acupuncture and acupressure have earned well-deserved reputations for being able to effectively relieve pain and many other disorders. In recent decades systems have been developed to help people self-clear their own trauma and stress by tapping on acupuncture points on their own body with their fingertips. The best known system for this is called EFT, or Emotional Freedom Technique. There are free instructions for doing EFT online[52]. A very useful guide is also the book *Energy Tapping for Trauma* by Gallo[53].

---

52 See http://www.emofree.com/eft-tutorial/tapping-basics/what-is-eft.html
53 Gallo, Fred, Energy Tapping for Trauma, New Harbinger Publications 2007

An EFT session consists of a person tapping on a series of acu-points on their face, chest and hands while breathing deeply. This can be combined with speaking affirmative or clearing statements. When I have needed to clear my own stress, as described in the story above, I have found that a combination of energy tapping with the simple eye movement method described below called IRT has really done the trick.

Practice 11-1: Instructions for Using Energy Tapping – Basic Procedure

1. Think about a painful or distressing issue, or feel it in your body. Rate your current distress on a scale of 0 – 10. 0 represents no distress, 10 is the worst it has been for you. If it is too difficult for you to rate the distress you can just assume you are at a "10" and go from there. Your aim will be to bring down this number by tapping and/or eye movements.

2. While breathing deeply, tap the points on the diagrams on the next two pages using the tips of your middle three fingers. It is fine to alternate your hands as you do the tapping. The points are usually tapped starting on the head, then on the chest and finishing on the hands.

3. Spend 3 – 5 minutes tapping, then rest and re-assess where you are on the scale of 0 - 10. In most cases the number should be lower.

4. If needed, do another round of tapping, then assess again. Continue until the score is as low as you can get it.

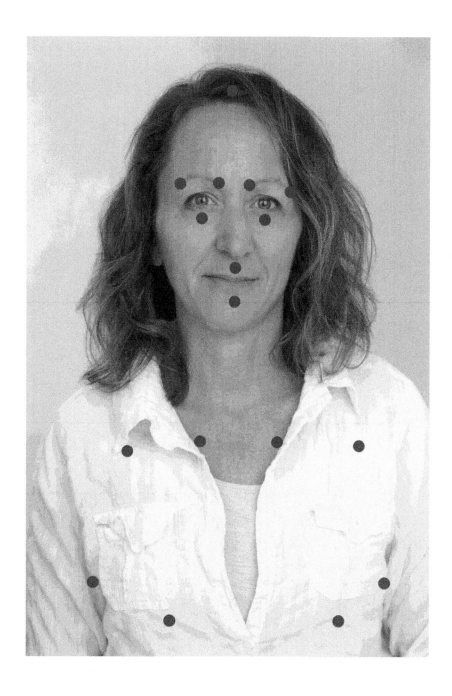

Commonly Used Energy Tapping Points

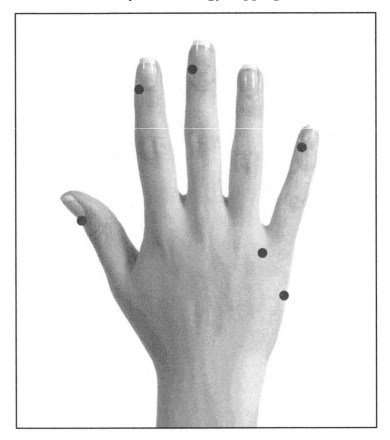

Energy Tapping Hand Points

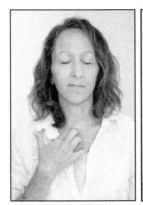 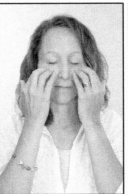 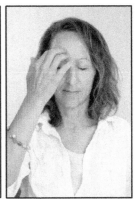

Energy Tapping

Some Considerations:

If after doing a few rounds of tapping you are not feeling much better, and your score is not significantly decreasing you may be dealing with switching or psychological reversal. Here are some simple techniques for neutralizing these blockages and getting into the groove:

Cross-body technique to get un-switched

1. While you are sitting down place your left ankle over your right ankle.

2. Put your arms in front of you with the backs of your hands touching each other. Without moving your left hand put your right hand over your left hand so your palms are touching in front of you with your right wrist over your left wrist. Interlace your fingers in that position. Then lower your arms and then raise them to that your interlocked hands rest over your heart.

3. At the same time place the tip of your tongue on the roof of your mouth, right behind your two front teeth.

4. Hold these positions while breathing deeply for a few minutes. This will usually reduce switching and allow you to gain more benefit from the energy tapping.

Cross-body technique

REDUCING PSYCHOLOGICAL REVERSAL

Psychological reversal happens when another issue you are not focusing on is blocking your attempts to clear the issue you are working on. Try this:

1. Use the pinky (ulnar) side of one of your hands to karate chop the palm of your other hand repeatedly.

2. While you do the karate chop movements make statements like this out loud with strong intent:

- *"Even though I (acknowledge the specific issue) I deeply and completely accept myself."*

Here are some examples:

- *"Even though I feel angry about Susan I deeply and completely accept myself."*
- *"Even though I feel scared and nervous I deeply and completely accept myself."*
- *"Even though my body aches and I can't sleep I deeply and completely accept myself and I release the pain."*

For more details on these methods see the reference works mentioned above[54].

---

54 See the two reference works listed in footnotes 52 and 53 earlier in this chapter.

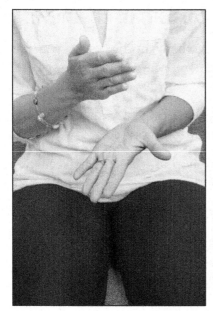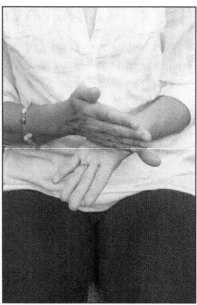

Hand tapping for psychological reversal

EMDR

In 1987 a woman suffering with traumatic memories named Francine Shapiro discovered how certain types of eye movements helped her to alleviate her distressed feelings. She did years of research on this and created a therapeutic system called EMD, or Eye Movement Desensitization. This name was later changed to EMDR, or Eye Movement Desensitization and Reprocessing[55].

EMDR has been proven to be effective for the alleviation of the distressing symptoms of PTSD in hundreds of research studies[56] A study from 1995 reported an 84% success rate in helping people

55 Shapiro, F. (1995). Eye Movement Desensitization and Reprocessing: Basic Principles, Protocols and Procedures (1st edition). New York: Guilford Press, also http://www.emdr.com/history-of-emdr/

56 Söndergaard, Hans Peter; Elofsson, Ulf, Psychophysiological Studies of EMDR Journal of EMDR Practice and Research, Volume 2, Number 4, 2008, pp. 282-288(7)

who had a single traumatic experience gain relief from the painful memory.[57]

In typical EMDR sessions a trained therapist moves an object back and forth in front of a patient's face and asks him to track the movement with his eyes while keeping his head still. The therapist will guide the client in recalling traumatic memories and impressions while doing these eye movements. This is usually combined with other therapeutic activities.

There are various theories about how and why EMDR works. One states that moving the eyes back and forth uses up much of the brain's energy resources that could otherwise be fueling traumatic feelings. By thinking of the painful memories while moving the eyes much of the energy and power of the memories can be diffused. Another theory says that EMDR is a lot like the rapid eye movements (REM) that happen during sleep. REM sleep helps resolve inner conflicts by replaying them, and so this theory holds that a similar process happens in the wakeful state with EMDR.

In this chapter I will share a simple method integrating eye movement with belief reprogramming that you can do for yourself to help diffuse and resolve uncomfortable or traumatic experiences. What I am offering here is not the full clinical system of EMDR, but a simpler offshoot given to clients to practice at home. It is called IRT or Immediate Release Technique. I don't see IRT only as a way to "make the bad feelings go away". In the larger view of healing it is an effective tool for loving and re-owning wounded parts of yourself.

Practice 11-2: Immediate Release Technique™ (IRT)

Start by practicing simple body-centered mindfulness (*see Chapter 10*). Invoke and tune into your higher Self in any way that you are comfortable with. (you will receive more guidance on doing this in subsequent chapters).

57 http://consults.blogs.nytimes.com/2012/03/02/the-evidence-on-e-m-d-r/?_r=0

Become aware of a painful or distressing feeling or memory you want to work with, and notice where it is focused within your body. Your body is the gateway of healing, and **if you want to heal you need to feel.** Therefore this step is vital. It is helpful to put the palm of one hand over the body area you are drawn to and offer yourself loving touch there.

Do your best to move out of mind-centered judgments, complaints and other "stories" about the painful feelings. Simply be willing to directly experience the bodily sensations and breathe into them. If you are aware of multiple painful issues choose the one that has been most distressing for you recently and focus on the sensations associated with it.

Ask yourself how painful or uncomfortable this feeling is on a scale of 0 – 10. 0 would be no discomfort and 10 represents the worst it has ever been for you. Remember or record that number.

Once you have rated the emotional pain, think about what limiting beliefs you may have that are associated with those feelings. For example, if a person you want to get to know seems to reject you and that brings up a painful emotional reaction, ask yourself what core belief you have about that. Core beliefs around rejection could include

"people just don't like me"

"I am unloveable"

"I always fail or blow it in relationships"

…and so on.

Once you get clear on what the belief is, write it in your journal. You will come back to replace this with a positive belief after the initial eye movement.

Then follow these steps:

1. Sit or stand and look straight ahead. If you can, touch your chin with your other hand to hold your head steady so it does not move

(after some practice of eye movement you won't need to do this anymore).

2. Breathe deeply and rapidly turn your eyes all the way to your left, then all the way to your right. Continue sweeping your eyes back and forth like windshield wipers while keeping your head still. As you do this blink your eyes rapidly and make sure you are breathing deeply. Sweep your eyes back and forth for at least a minute while blinking and breathing, then rest. As you do the eye movements, keep bringing your focus back into the core of the painful feelings in your body.

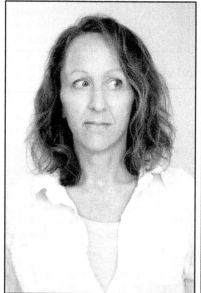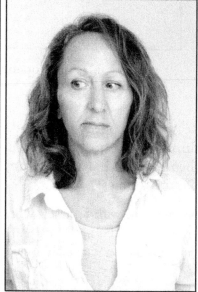

IRT eye movement

3. After you are complete with the eye movements open your eyes as wide as you can, then clench your eyes, face and mouth closed. Alternate between open and closed face four times.

IRT open and closed face

4. After the open and closed facial movements breathe in deeply through your nose to fill your body with air as fully as possible, then blow all the air out through your mouth as fully as possible. Do this 4 times.

5. Check in with yourself where the feelings you were focusing on are now on the scale of 0 – 10. Has there been any change? It is very helpful to journal about what you experienced.

What I just described is the simplest form of eye movement self-healing. You can also experiment with moving your eyes in other directions other than just left and right. Other possibilities are diagonally to the upper left, lower left, upper right or lower right, or straight up and straight down. Each of these activates a different part of the brain. Just be spontaneous in these eye movement directions, and stay sensitive to how each one makes you feel.

Once you complete the eye movement procedure repeat it. You can either go further in releasing more of the same uncomfortable/traumatic feeling or focus on a different one. If you choose to work with another painful feeling, check in about where it is focused within your body, as the location may be different. Check your 0 – 10 scale and repeat the five steps above.

Once you feel you have gotten the maximum benefit from doing the eye movements and your 0 – 10 score is as low as possible, it is important to replace the painful belief or memory with a positive, empowering impression. Here is a great way to do that:

Remember the limiting belief you originally had about the painful experience. Use that in making these healing statements:

> **Statement One:** It is my intention, as the master being that I am, to release my beliefs in the reasons why (insert limiting belief here, such as "I am unloveable" or "life is a weary struggle")

> **Statement Two:** I now totally accept and believe that I am (put the opposite of the limiting belief here, or any positive belief you would LIKE to have about this part of your life. For example "I am loved and cherished" or "I live in abundance, always")

> **Statement Three:** I now totally accept and believe that I can have joy in my life, and I am perfect, just the way I am (this statement is the same regardless of the beliefs you are working with!)

You can empower this positive re-programming by using lazy 8 eye movements. Move your eyes to follow an imaginary 8 on its side. See diagram below. Go in one direction for a couple of minutes, then switch direction. Think about your new positive belief while you do this.

If you are a kinesthetic "feeling" person feel the positive energy of the new belief. If you are more visual you can visualize an image or scene that reflects your new, positive belief about yourself. If your new belief is "I am loved and cherished" you can imagine a wonderful partner holding you and pouring love all over you, or something like that. If your new belief is that you are a successful event leader you can imagine yourself speaking to a large group of turned-on and highly appreciative students! Do the lazy 8 movement as you feel the feelings or visualize the image.

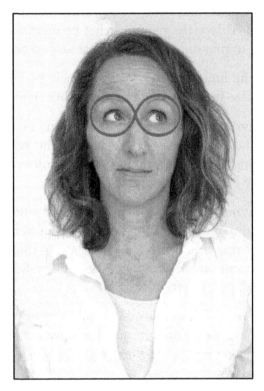

Lazy 8 eye movement

Here is an example of using these healing statements for reprogramming a belief about being unsafe associated with feelings of tightness and discomfort in the heart area:

Statement One: It is my intention, as the master being that I am, to release my beliefs in the reasons why I feel unsafe and vulnerable to being hurt again.

Statement Two: I now totally accept and believe that I am safe, confident and protected by the Divine.

Statement Three: I now totally accept and believe that I can have joy in my life, and I am perfect, just the way I am

After you go through a few rounds of eye movement and healing statements check in with yourself. How does your body feel now? What is your emotional state like? Are you in touch with your calm center? Where is the discomfort on the 0 – 10 scale? If you find you are feeling better express gratitude. If you still feel tight, pained or incomplete repeat the procedure, perhaps by working with a different belief, feeling or body area.

This is a simple, yet powerful system for inner self-healing. This procedure can be combined with tapping methods, such as EFT (Emotional Freedom Technique) [58]. Experiment with different combinations of eye movement, tapping and belief reprogramming.

Practice 11-3: Combining Energy Tapping with IRT

Once you get the hang of energy tapping and eye movement therapy you can combine them for increased effects. Simply tap the acu-pressure points shown in the diagrams on pages 137 and 138 in sequence while you rapidly sweep your eyes back and forth like windshield wipers. Breathe deeply while you do both of these. For maximum effectiveness verbally say what you are letting go. Here is an example of this combined self-clearing method.

This example is for a woman named Joan recovering after a painful relationship breakup with a man named Dylan. This

---

58 http://www.emofree.com/eft-tutorial/tapping-basics/how-to-do-eft.html

experience triggered traumatic memories of previous feelings of abandonment going back to her childhood.

1. Joan allows herself to deeply feel her emotional pain. She does her best to rate her pain on a scale of 0 – 10. She decides that it is a 10 or higher – it really hurts!

2. She starts tapping the series of acu-points shown in the diagrams, first using her right fingertips and later switching to her left fingertips.

3. As she does this she breathes deeply, even though a part of her would like to hold her breath and try to stop the painful feelings. But she is sick and tired enough of the pain to be willing to stretch her comfort zone and breathe deeply.

4. As she is tapping the points in sequence Joan starts moving her eyes back and forth like a rapid windshield wiper while blinking her eyes. She is careful to keep her head from moving. She does this by using the hand she is not using for tapping to steady her chin. That way the value of the eye movements is maximized.

5. While tapping and moving her eyes Joan speaks about what she is letting go of out loud:

"I am blinking and breathing out this big pain in my heart"
"I am tapping out my anguish and suffering."
"I am blinking and breathing out my rage toward Dylan."
"I am tapping and blinking out my terror."
"I am blinking and breathing out wanting to run away and get drunk"

6. After 3 – 5 minutes of all this she stops to re-evaluate. If her score has dropped from 10 down to 7 or lower she is on the right track. She can do another round of tapping and eye movement to create deeper relief, or to work on another aspect of her pain.

If her score has not gone down much, Joan can try the cross-body technique to eliminate switching or the karate chop on the hand technique to clear psychological reversal. After trying these she can go back to a few more rounds of tapping and eye movements.

7. After Joan has gotten her distress score down as low as possible (hopefully down to a 1 or 2) it will be highly beneficial for her to do practices to tune into and enjoy her calm center. These are presented in Chapter 12. If she can chill out enough to just be there and relax into her own inner space of peace and self-love she will gain the maximum healing and soothing benefit[59].

Combining energy tapping with IRT

Energy tapping and eye movement self-healing are effective tools for helping you manage your own feelings and moods. This is a vital part of personal healing and taking charge of your life. These practices could help you reduce or eliminate the need for

---

[59] See Chapter 10 for guidance on finding your calm center within your breath.

psychotropic medications such as anti-anxiety and anti-depressive drugs. If you choose to do this, wean yourself off them with the support of your doctor.

Sometimes self-care practices are not enough, and you might need more powerful methods offered by a specially trained professional. In Chapter 15 you will learn about the TERS system that works in a similar way as EMDR, but can be much more rapidly effective. TERS combines vibrational energy therapies and stimulation of acupuncture points with desensitization procedures. While the proponents of EMDR state that each traumatic memory is likely to require at least 5 hours of therapy, TERS has been shown to permanently deprogram a major traumatic memory within one 40 minute session.

12

Reclaiming Your Calm Center: Breathwork

Feelings come and go like clouds in a windy sky.
Conscious breathing is my anchor.
-- THICT NHAT HANH

There are a multitude of meditative and transformative practices focusing on the breath. Most involve some form of conscious breathing or breath control in order to create a shift in the body or mind. These include pranayama, kundalini yoga, rebirthing, Qi Gong and sexual tantric practices.

This chapter contains three simple practices for opening the flow of energy in your body, awakening your consciousness and cultivating your deeper enjoyment of life. These practices are carefully selected for their power and simplicity. They are:

1. *7-7-7 Breathing* – a simple breath practice ideal for helping beginning meditators develop their concentration and experience the rewards of meditation right away. Doing this rapidly brings you into a centered, grounded awareness and can boost your energy and vitality.

---

2. *Mindfulness of breath* – A variation of the mindfulness practices taught in Chapter 10. A great way to go through life!

3. *Anapana* – Sitting meditation on the inflow and outflow of breath. Of all the practices taught in this book, anapana meditation is probably the one with the greatest power to clear negativity and blockages in your deep mind (*samskaras*) and permanently transform your life for the better.

Of these three practices, only the first one includes breath control. The other two are for cultivating conscious awareness of your natural breath.

Here is a "secret" for getting the most benefit from all these practices – train yourself to keep the tip of your tongue on the roof of your mouth as much of the time as possible. Also try to keep it there whenever you are not talking, eating or kissing. The method and reasons for this are thoroughly explained in *Chapter 9*.

Let's start with a bit of insight and science about your breath.

THE POWER OF BREATH

Breath is our direct connection to spirit, our true Self or divine source. Our language confirms this. The word "spirit" is derived from the ancient Latin word *spiritus* which means breath or spirit. We call breathing in *inspiration* and breathing out *expiration*. The word inspiration also means "something that makes someone want to do something or that gives someone an idea about what to do or create" or "the excitement of the mind or emotions to a high level of feeling or activity". We also use the term expiration to refer to the time of death, when the spirit leaves the body.

While most of us take breathing for granted it is our most precious asset. Every effective spiritual path or meditation system emphasizes the great value of mindful (conscious) breathing. In this chapter I will use the term *breathwork* to refer to conscious breath practices.

The functions of your body are classified as either *voluntary* or *involuntary*. Voluntary functions are those that you can control with your conscious mind. Picking up a teacup is a voluntary action because most people can decide to do that or not do it. The majority of movements of the large muscles of our body are voluntary. Involuntary functions are those that happen without the control of your conscious mind. Most of our vital life functions are involuntary, including your heartbeat, digestion, glandular action, cellular growth and repair (healing). It is a very good thing for our survival that these are involuntary. Imagine if you had to remember to do all of those things!

Breath is one of the few bodily functions that is both voluntary and involuntary. As long as you are alive breath will move in and out of your body without you having to think about it. Yet you also have the option to regulate or control your breath with your mind to a considerable extent. You can hold your breath, speed it up, slow it down or breathe in special patterns. These are all forms of breath control, and have often been used for rejuvenation or health benefits.

The most advanced system of breath control is the science of *pranayama* from India. Its purpose is control and augmentation of the body's energy flows using breathwork. Practitioners of this and other related activities are called *yogis*. By practicing pranayama yogis have been able to boost their vitality and put their minds into deep states of meditation.

Practicing some advanced forms of pranayama have also empowered people to do what would seem like superhuman feats. These are called *siddhis* or special powers. Dedicated yogis have reportedly developed siddhis that include melting snow with their scantily clothed bodies, lifting objects much heavier than people could ordinarily lift and being able to understand the language of animals. I'll tell you the most important *siddhi* you can develop for yourself − that is to reclaim the power to feel whole and good in your own body. For modern people experiencing low-grade PTSD (or worse) this is a major empowerment.

155

Breathing deeply is the sign of a free person. The most important practice of all is to breathe fully and consciously, and to do this as much as you possibly can throughout your life.

Here is why. Research has shown that deep breathing has beneficial, strengthening or healing effects on the:

- Heart
- Brain
- Digestive system
- Energy production systems of the body
- Immune system
- Acid-alkaline balance (ph)
- It has also been shown to help relieve or reduce:
- Asthma
- Chronic obstructive pulmonary disease
- Excess stress hormones
- High blood pressure
- Anxiety

Full breathing stimulates the *vagus nerve*, which runs from the base of the brain into the abdomen. When activated the vagus nerve releases *acetylcholine*, a neuro-transmitter that increases focus and calmness. Stimulation of the vagus nerve also helps relieve depression.

Deep breathing also balances the autonomic nervous system – the overall regulator for all the involuntary functions of our body. It has been shown to increase alertness and the relaxation response. To put the cherry on top of the sundae, deep breathing has also been shown to have rejuvenating, anti-aging effects.

Breathing in (inspiration) slightly increases your heart rate. Breathing out (expiration) slightly slows down the heart. So accentuating the outbreath is one of the best ways to calm your heart if you are feeling anxious. Another way of saying this is that the outbreath activates the parasympathetic side of your autonomic nervous system, and this induces relaxation and calm in the organs.

BREATH, EMOTIONS AND YOUR CALM CENTER

That's the physical level. Let's look at the consciousness level. Think about healthy children. They are usually full of energy and may be even be rambunctious. Their bodies are generally more relaxed than adults. They don't tend to hold onto so much tension. They get angry or upset and then just as quickly they let it go and move on. Healthy children tend to breathe fully.

Now think about other children who have been abused and who have grown up in frequent fear. They are afraid to speak their truth and have secrets they are not allowed to tell. They are often tiptoeing around for fear of being hurt, criticized or abused. A young child cannot run away because she is dependent on her caregivers. So she may attempt to protect herself by making herself smaller and less noticeable. The number one way to do this is to breathe in a shallow way. Why? Because this is part of the physiology of fear and avoidance of hurt.

Think about an animal that is trying to hide from a predator. If it cannot run away it will try to be as still and small and quiet as possible. To do this it slows its breath way down and makes it as shallow as possible. If you are ever hiding from a predator making yourself still and small may be a good plan. But not a good way to live day in and day out.

Breathing in a shallow way goes along with a long term feeling of fear. You may not be thinking you are in a state of fear. But deep in your subconscious mind and cellular memory you may have a feeling that the world is not safe. You may deeply believe that you can't afford to really show yourself and be powerful. If you want to shift this pattern of giving your power away and being small know that breathing deeply is the sign of a free and empowered person. Even if you don't read any of the other practices in this section, and you took to heart this guidance about expanding your ability to breathe deeply, your life could change for the better.

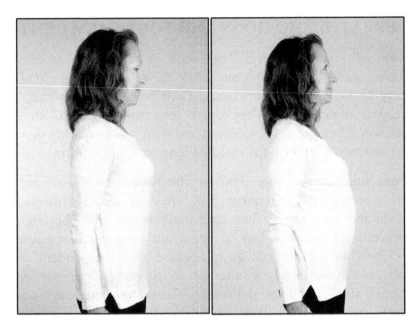

Belly breathing

As you breathe more deeply let your body respond to the new level of breath and oxygen. Follow what your body tells you. You may feel like stretching more. You may get urges to get up and walk more often, especially if you do a lot of desk work. You may crave getting outdoors and hiking more. You may think about something you want to say to someone that really needs to be said, and that the shallow breathing part of you was afraid to say. Follow these urges. It will be very healthy and empowering for you, and it all starts with the breath.

I have trained myself to go to my calm center in all kinds of situations. I go to my breath to find my calm center when I need to concentrate. I go to my calm center when I want to relax. I go to my calm center when I need to bring myself into the Now moment. I go to my calm center when I am confronted with challenging, stressful experiences, and it makes a world of difference. I go to my calm center when I am craving intimacy and connection, and want to touch my source of love. This all happens through the breath.

Learning to be in my calm center has been a safe haven for me and it can be for you. I can clearly see that being in conscious communion with my calm center is more than just comforting. It has been a survival factor during emergencies. If I had panicked during some challenging situations I have been in things could have gone much worse.

BREATH PRACTICES

Practice 12-1: 7-7-7 Breathing

This practice has many benefits:
- Balancing the autonomic nervous system
- Bringing your attention into your calm center
- Quieting the mind
- Preparing you for any form of meditation
- Helping doctors and healers focus their healing energies
- It is simple

Instructions

1. Create your intention to do this practice
2. Touch the tip of your tongue lightly to the roof of your mouth, behind your front teeth.
3. Close your mouth and breathe in through your nose while you silently count to 7.
4. After your in-breath, hold your breath for the count of 7
5. Open your mouth and exhale through it for the count of 7
6. Repeat for at least one minute. Doing this practice for five to ten minutes or more will provide the best results.

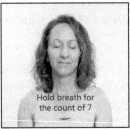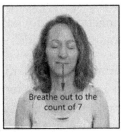

7-7-7 breathing

Find your own pace. If it is easy for you to hold your breath, count more slowly. If that is harder for you count a little faster. If you have breathing problems and a count of 7 is too much, simply reduce the count to 3 - 3 - 3, or 4 - 4 - 4. Once you get comfortable doing that, you can gradually increase the counts until you get up to 7 – 7 – 7. As stated earlier there are tremendous health benefits to increasing your breathing capacity, and building your ability to expand your counts in this practice will help you do that.

Practice 12-2: Mindfulness of Breath

You can train yourself to stay aware of your breath in the background of your attention, as you are going through all your daily experiences. This will also bring you vast physical and psychological benefits.

The first step is to create an intention to stay aware of your breath more each day. Then bring your awareness back to the experience of breathing over and over again until it becomes a habit. It doesn't matter if you are "good" or "bad" at doing this! Just understand the value of reclaiming your calm center and persist, no matter what it takes. You will succeed eventually because this is your true nature.

12-2-A: Preparing for Mindfulness of Breath

To get started with this practice I recommend that you first discover more about your habitual relationship with breathing. Sit in front of a mirror wearing as few clothes as possible, and put a notebook and pen in front of you so you have a way to record your experience. Breathe in the way you normally would. Don't try to change your normal breathing pattern yet. This means leaving it on automatic, **involuntary** control. Now notice – are you breathing mostly in your chest, or are you breathing mostly in your lower abdomen? Is your breath deep or is it shallow? As you observe how you have been breathing ask yourself what experiences are associated with your breath patterns. What feelings, attitudes or memories come up as you do that? Reflect on them and record those in your notebook.

Now consciously choose to breathe more deeply. Take the reins for **voluntary** breath control. Breathe in through your nose. First feel your chest rise, then direct the breath to balloon out your lower abdomen. Then breathe out through your mouth in the reverse order, letting your belly contract and then your chest fall. Really accentuate the depth of your breath. Look at yourself in the mirror. How does it feel to be seen, to be larger in life? Observe yourself from your Witness consciousness. Is it easy or difficult for you to breathe more fully? Do any thoughts or feelings arise as you do it? Without judging your experience in any way record these.

12-2-B: Mindfulness of Breath Practice

After doing this self-observation a few times by yourself practice start breathing consciously when you are around other people. Intend to remember to breathe more deeply in all your encounters and say to yourself "I am a free man or woman. I am choosing to be fully alive". Notice what comes up. Stay with it, keeping an attitude of self-love. Keep challenging your old decision to be small and breathe shallowly.

Try going through your day breathing freely and fully. Try putting little sticky notes around your home and car to remind you. As you do this you may notice that you want to drink more water, eat different foods, release some toxic relationships from your life or do more activities that strengthen and invigorate your body.

This is an extremely powerful practice. When you change your breathing pattern you are changing yourself at the core. As you change your breathing you will change the wiring of your brain and nervous system. Your autonomic nervous system will regain a healthier balance between sympathetic (activation) and parasympathetic (relaxation and rest). You are literally re-wiring your physiology. This will gradually transform the damage that was done due to trauma and bring you into your calm center more of the time. You are tapping into the neuro-plasticity of your brain and nervous system. They will adapt to the new breathing pattern.

DEALING WITH RESISTANCE OR REACTION

Don't be surprised if you feel resistance come up within you as you start changing your breathing patterns. This resistance often takes the form of procrastination or avoidance of actually doing the meditation, or the mind's tendency to frequently space out when you do practice.

There could be a whole hierarchy of inner voices and subpersonalities in you dedicated to keeping you in the box, in a more limited state. Why? Because one of our greatest urges is to try to be safe. As a child you did the best you could do to survive. The negative side of neuroplasticity is that your brain may have adapted to adverse conditions in a way that created shallow breathing and a possible host of other survival mechanisms. These could include stooped body posture, asthma, stuttering, dissociation (spacing out), fear of intimacy and touch, feeling emotionally numb, violently acting out and much more.

Again, this is the tragedy of PTSD. While it may have been necessary for a small child in an abusive family to breathe shallowly and create these coping mechanisms to avoid unwelcome attention that is no longer a useful strategy when he becomes an adult.

If uncomfortable emotions do come up as you practice conscious, deeper breathing that make it difficult for you to continue you can try *pendulating* in and out of those feelings. This means gently allowing the painful feelings to come up, then step back from the practice for a while to regroup and center yourself. Then go back in. You go back in by breathing deeply with courage and determination to be whole. Continue to affirm "I am a free and powerful person".

If opening up your breath and life force feels overwhelming to do by yourself please reach out for support from trusted friends or professionals. This is far better than retreating back into what may have seemed like a "safer" denial of your aliveness. Those overwhelming or difficult feelings could be a gateway into an expanded, more fulfilling phase of your life once you get the support you need to persist in these practices.

Practice 12-3: Anapana Meditation

Anapana, the practice of observing breath moving in and out of the nostrils, was taught by the Buddha as a primary form of meditation recommended to his students. According to Buddhist scriptures this is also what he personally practiced as he went through his own process of enlightenment.[60].

Here is a step-by-step guide for practicing anapana:

1. Choose a place: Find a quiet place for meditation where you will not be disturbed.

---

[60] Anapana was the first meditation taught by the Buddha, as written about in the *Maha-satipatthana Sutta*, the Great Discourse on the Foundations of Mindfulness.

2 Find your comfortable position: Choose a method to support you in sitting up straight. Common options are:

A. Sitting on a yoga mat in a lotus or half-lotus position, or with cushions under your rear end. Use as many cushions as you need to sit up comfortably with spine erect.

Lotus position　　　　　**Sitting on cushion**

B. Sitting on a straight-backed chair. My favorite meditation position is sitting up in a straight-backed chair with thin pillows on the seat of the chair, rolled behind my back and on the floor under my feet.

Meditating on chair

C. Using a meditation bench.

Meditation bench

Experiment with these options until you find one that is comfortable for you, and will allow you to sit still.

It is vital that you sit up with your spine erect during anapana practice. It is extremely difficult to develop the required concentration if you are lying down or leaning back into a soft sofa. Intend to sit as still as possible as you practice. If this is difficult for you at first do the best you can, and gradually increase your ability to sit as you get more comfortable with the practice.

3. Hand position: Place your hands in a comfortable position you can maintain for the length of the practice. The traditional hand position for this is placing one hand on your lap with palm facing up, and the other hand palm up on top of the first hand. Placing your hands palm up on your knees with thumbs and index fingertips touching is also beneficial. See the photos below.

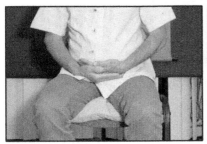
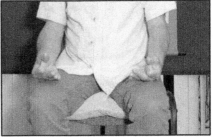

Palm mudra   **Hand mudra**

4. Use a timer: Set a timer for your chosen duration of practice. All smart phones have alarm clocks as a standard function, and these work well. You can also purchase other inexpensive digital timers. Just make sure the timer is silent during operation. It is best to start by setting your timer for a minimum of 10 minutes. Work up to longer practice times. You will receive much more benefit from longer practice periods, but any amount is valuable.

Using a timer is recommended because without one it is likely that your mind will chatter about how much time is left, or worry that you are missing something by taking too long. By using a timer you can train yourself to let go of all that concern and relax more deeply into the practice.

5. Mouth: Close your mouth and keep it closed for the duration of the practice. I recommend that you touch the tip of your tongue to the roof of your mouth and keep it there as much as you can during anapana practice[61].

6. Where to focus: Put your full attention right under your nose. The area of concentration includes the space immediately under your nostrils and the skin area above your upper lip. Simply observe the physical flow of breath in this limited space

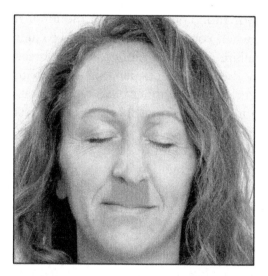

Anapana area of concentration

Watch the breath flow in and out. Don't try to control the breath in any way. The key is to observe your natural **involuntary** flow of breath. It is involuntary breath that connects your conscious awareness to your deep sub-conscious mind. This is a major key to the power of this practice.

7. Keep coming back: Each time you become aware that your mind has wandered simply bring it back to the flow of breath. Do

[61] This is not part of the Buddha's instructions, but it sure works for me to augment the feeling of self-connection and concentration

not criticize yourself for having lost concentration. Such reactions could create new samskaras. Keep bringing your attention back to your breath **patiently** and **persistently**.

8. Close practice: When you hear your meditation timer sound, end the practice. Of course if you wish to practice longer, do so.

SOME TIPS AND CONSIDERATIONS FOR ANAPANA PRACTICE

1. You cannot fail: The tendency of the inner mental critic is to criticize you when your mind wanders, and to judge your degree or success or failure at concentrating on your breath. Forget about all that! The benefit of anapana is not about how well you concentrate or how much inner peace you feel. It is only about the process of bringing your mind back to your breath over and over again even if it wanders. It is about your steady commitment to sitting for a definite amount of time on a regular basis, and making the effort to gradually build your inner concentration. It does not matter how strong or weak your concentration seems to be. It is never useful to compare yourself to anyone else in your ability to meditate.

You are in the perfect place right now for doing your anapana practice. It is a lot like walking on a path. You can only be where you are on the path, and then take one step after another to move forward. It is the same way with anapana. Where you are in your degree of concentration and enjoyment of inner peace is unimportant. What is important is accepting your experience and your determination to do the practice regularly. That is what will gradually heal your mind.

2. Regularity is the key to success: Do your best to choose one or two times per day for practice that are as regular as possible. Meditating twice a day is best. Right after you wake up and before bed are great times. If you are too sleepy to meditate right before bed, then choose a time in the late afternoon or early evening when you are alert. You will likely find that whatever activity you do after meditating will be more enjoyable. When I lived in San Antonio, Texas during the 1970's my friends and I would meditate before going out dancing on weekend nights. With clear minds and hearts we had much more fun!

3. The power in the pause: As you get comfortable with anapana practice you will be able to relax into your breath more and more. As you do that it is likely that you will notice brief pauses between your breaths. When the body is relaxed there will be a tiny pause after you breathe in and before you breathe out. There is another pause after you breathe out and before you breathe in. Noticing and relaxing into these pauses deepens your experience.

Those pauses between the breaths are times when you can most directly tap into your true Self, the divine within you. This is the experience of no-thing, what has been called Tao, God or Universal Source. For most of us our ego-based mind has filled these sacred spaces between the breaths with random, fear-based thoughts. Anapana practice will help you clear these spaces so you can enjoy your inner connection.

As mentioned in *Chapter 11*, many traditional stories and myths tell about a hero coming back to his homeland and finding it overrun with enemies or demons[62]. The hero must fight to clear them away so he can take charge again and restore proper order to his homeland. I believe many of these stories are external images of our inner work. As we do anapana we can reduce useless thinking and better experience the clear spaces within our breath. As we reclaim our calm center through this practice our mind heals and our heart can blossom.

4. Let release happen: As you commit to regular anapana practice it is likely that you will go through a process of unwinding, or psychic housecleaning. This can take many forms. Some examples: old memories resurfacing, strange or disturbing dreams, unexplainable welling up of joy and tranquility, energy/mood swings or bodily symptoms of sickness that arise and then disappear quickly. If any of these come up as you commit to your anapana practice rejoice! This is validation that your meditation practice is working! You are lightening up your load of samskara and getting free. Don't be attached positively or negatively to any of these experiences, just bless them and let them go. Keep breathing deeply and taking good care of yourself.

I recommend that you read or re-read *Chapter 6, The Universal Path* as you start practicing anapana. This will give you a deeper appreciation of how and why you release psychic "gunk" as you commit to a regular meditation practice.

5. Practice equanimity: Don't have any expectations about how you will experience anapana meditation. Don't judge how much "psychic housecleaning" you are having. According to the teachings of the Buddha inner suffering (samskara) is created through our reactions of craving and aversion to the sensations of life. This also applies to meditation.

---

[62] Two of my favorite stories of this kind are in the Greek myth the Odyssey, and in the final book of The Lord of the Rings by J.R.R. Tolkien. The new Wonder Woman movie of 2017 also illustrates this archetypal story beautifully.

If you "crave" peaceful, relaxing sensations in meditation or have "aversion" to times when you feel fidgety, mentally overactive or otherwise uncomfortable you are missing the point of the practice. The point is not to strive for a peaceful experience. The purpose of meditation is to develop mental equanimity by patiently and persistently doing the technique of anapana regardless of how you experience it. This is sometimes hard to grasp for those of us Type A, goal-oriented Western meditators!

6. Using a mantra: The greatest benefit of anapana comes from practicing it in its pure, original form as described above, where you only focus on the breath. If you are starting out with this practice and find it very difficult to concentrate you can add the use of a mantra to the concentration on the breath. This is a lot like using training wheels on a bicycle when introducing bike riding to a young child. It is useful for giving her initial confidence, but can be removed as soon as she gains her own balance.

One of the most powerful mantras is I AM. It is the most true statement you can make in words! You can combine it with anapana. As you breathe in silently say *"I"*. As you breathe out silently say *"AM"*. The sound of the breath is much like that, you are just accentuating it with your mind.

7 – 7 – 7 breathing, as presented in practice 11-1 is another great way to gain confidence in your ability to meditate. It is also a great, user-friendly tool for everyday life.

Once you feel steady in using either of these methods try to transition to anapana practice without any counting or use of mantra.

Practice 12-4: Mindfulness of Your Calm Center

Doing any of these breathwork practices regularly will train your mind to stay consciously connected with your calm center more and more of the time. Here are a few additional instructions for tuning into inner peace:

•Put the tip of your tongue on the roof of your mouth, behind your two front teeth.

•Start with your anapana breath practice. As you settle into the focus on your natural breath create an intention to feel your calm center. Say something like this: "It is my intention to feel (or deepen my experience of) my calm center."

• With your attention on your breath consciously relax your body, especially your chest area. Connect with the part of you that longs for inner peace. Allow that part to tune into the good feeling in your breath. People who are experienced meditators should find this easy. If you feel a lot of tension and discomfort in your body you can still find this good feeling in your breath, but it may take patience and repeated practice. Don't give up. If you need help remember that receiving healing sessions or meditating in dedicated groups can help you get in touch with your calm center more quickly and easily.

• Once you connect with the calm center of your breath enjoy it. Relax into it. Get to know this place within. Hang out there and get cozy with it. Remember, keeping the tip of your tongue on the roof of your mouth empowers you to connect more readily.

To make this easier I have created a practice video called *Mindfulness and Self-Love* on my website. You can access it at http://drstarwynn.com/videos/

PUTTING IT ALL TOGETHER

Reclaiming your calm center is a process. There is nothing you can do that is more valuable or rewarding than this. I will repeat again – don't judge whether you are "good" or "bad" at doing these practices. Just put one proverbial foot in front of the other and do them. Remember that you don't have to create or conjure up your calm center. It is already there, always has been and always will be. Isn't that a relief?

Your job is to gradually wean yourself away from all the weapons of mass distraction that have been seducing your attention away from what is real, and keep bringing it back to the Self. Not to some idealization of the Self, not to any belief about it, but to the simple, nurturing experience you will find within your breath. Be patient and kind with yourself and invoke your inner Warrior who will not back down.

Why not do it right now?

13

Self-Love and Self Forgiveness

Self-love is the source of all our other loves
-- *PIERRE CORNEILLE*

THE HARDEST FORM OF LOVE

There are so many people who have been exploring various systems of healing and psychotherapy for years or decades. They have read loads of inspirational and self-help books. Many of them have studied with a succession of mentors and teachers. Through all this they have learned a lot about themselves and how the Universe works. Most have also made it a priority to nurture loving relationships with friends, partners, children, animals or God. Yet after all this there still remains one major missing piece for most of them. That missing piece is self-love.

After observing this in countless people I have known, and noticing it in myself, I can only conclude that loving ourselves fully and unconditionally is the hardest form of love to come by. It is also the most important and the most powerful healer that there is.

It is our false beliefs about ourselves and lack of self-love that open the door for buggy stress programs to pollute our calm center.

Ultimately self-love is the thing you have to do first and foremost. It is generally easier to love yourself or others when you are happy and things are going well. Love is our true nature and it flows naturally when we are feeling good. Most people find it harder to love when they are feeling emotional pain. Yet that is precisely when love is needed the most.

The first step of self-love is to sit with your pain. Feel your reactions, emotions, sensations, impulses, urges, frustrations. Where are they stemming from? Where do you feel it in your body? If you get rejected, what is your go-to reaction? What's the first thought that crosses your mind? That uncomfortable feeling that results is YOU. Take a beat. Sit with it. Feel it caressing through your veins. Be your pain. Send love to that area. And guess what? You felt the reaction, and no one died. You survived it. You're a powerful being and you can survive even the worst insult. It hurts, yes. But if you love yourself, it will be ok.

This is what being conscious is all about: feeling those uncomfortable feelings, practicing forgiveness, self-love, self-acceptance, and then taking action from that place. This is at the core of mindfulness.

There is an intimate relationship between self-love and being in your calm center. These reinforce each other. The more you love yourself the more you will want to make the effort to be in your calm center, because that is the most loving way to be with yourself. The more you experience your calm center the easier it is to allow love to flow through your body. The simple breath practices taught in *Chapter 12, Reclaiming Your Calm Center* come much more naturally when you are loving yourself.

Some people I have talked with actually believe it is wrong to deeply love themselves. They have been trained to see this as a form of conceit. Don't believe that! That is one more ignorant message to keep people down and disempowered. Conceitedness, narcissism and self-centeredness are really cover-ups for LACK of self-love.

Many people seem to have good self-esteem and are able to achieve a lot, but at their core they are not really comfortable being with themselves. Most of us go to great lengths to stay busy with activities that keep us distracted from fully being with our own inner feelings.

There is nothing wrong with reading the newspaper, watching TV, staying busy with activities and goals, having your senses stimulated and enjoying the company of friends, lovers and family. These are all healthy human activities. But if these were all taken away – how comfortable would you be simply being with yourself? If there was no one to give you love and validation and nothing to distract you from simply being with you, could you enjoy it?

In prisons the worst punishment is solitary confinement. This is torture for people who don't love themselves. When all the external stimulation is taken away they can't escape from the self-condemning and fearful voices in their heads.

Please enjoy a story many of us heard in our childhoods to illustrate this point.

If you are anywhere near as old as me you no doubt remember the folklore story of Brer Rabbit and the Tar Baby created by Uncle Remus.

In that story Brer Rabbit – a happy go lucky creature – came across a figure made out of tar who did not respond properly to his greetings, even after repeating his greeting "Good Day Sir!". This got Brer Rabbit mad – because he was a proper Southern gentle rabbit who expected his courtesies returned. So he smacked that tar baby right proper and got himself stuck up real good with all that tar and could not free himself.

This was of course a trap laid by Brer Fox, who was hungry and looking to feast upon Brer Rabbit. Brer Fox came out of his hiding place and started musing about how to kill the trapped and helpless

Brer Rabbit. The prospect of finally killing the wily Brer Rabbit who had always escaped in the past by outsmarting him was a delicious thought.

Brer Rabbit and Brer Fox

Brer Fox started thinking aloud. He said "I think I'll skin you alive before I eat you."

Brer Rabbit replied "Sure, skin me alive if you must, but whatever you do, don't throw me in that yonder briar patch" (for those not familiar with that term, a briar patch is a clump of briar bushes with lots of sharp thorns in them).

So next Brer Fox said "Maybe I'll slowly burn you alive over a fire."

Brer Rabbit came back with "OK, skin me alive, burn me, but whatever you do, don't throw me in that briar patch!"

Brer Fox wasn't enjoying his victory enough yet, so he used his imagination further: "If those don't scare you, I think I'll drown you in the river."

Brer Rabbit retorted "OK, Brer Fox, you win. Skin me, burn me, drown me but please, please whatever you do don't throw me in that briar patch."

Brer Fox wanted to do the worst to Brer Rabbit, so he said "Well since you are so afraid of that briar patch, that's exactly what I'm going to do!" He pulled Brer Rabbit free from the tar baby and threw him right into that briar patch.

Brer Rabbit soon stuck his head out and derided his former captor by saying "thank you Brer Fox! I was born and bred in that briar patch!" and scampered off, free.

Remember that story? Anyway, what point do you think I am trying to make here about self-love?

It's likely that most of us can relate to Brer Rabbit. Our modern version of his request could be "That's OK, make me work two jobs, make me deal with loads of stress, make me jog five miles a day, make me drive my kids all over creation as Super Mom, make me work out at the gym for hours, but whatever you do, don't make me be with and love myself!!!"

The version for new age people could be more like this: "It's OK - make me do lots of difficult yoga poses, give me hours of volunteer service to do, make me face my inner demons, make me give up all the foods I enjoy, make me abstain from sex, make me max out my credit cards going to expensive retreats, I'll even be a Guru and lead thousands of people, but whatever you do, don't make me be with and love myself!!!"

Practicing meditation is a way to learn to enjoy being with your own core. Meditation is a process of bringing the mind inside over and over again. What I notice when I start meditation is that at first there is usually a lot of mental activity and random thoughts but eventually my mind relaxes and I start feeling the pleasure of my own inner space of breath and pure life force.

When I sit down to meditate my ego mind still often sounds like Brer Rabbit: "I'll take care of all those unanswered emails, I'll do more chores around the house, I'll do all those unfinished tasks, I'll do lots of service in my community, I'll make all those calls I have been putting off but PLEASE DON'T MAKE ME GET QUIET AND GO INSIDE MYSELF!!".

But here is the magic – once I do make the commitment to practice, in a short time I start feeling so good, and once again I realize "I was born and bred in this briar patch (inner self)".

What I am going to offer next is a very powerful form of meditation. It involves willingly stepping into your inner briar patch with love.

Practice 13-1: Brief Guided Meditation of Self-Connection

Sit down in a quiet place in which you can be in a meditative space. Take some time to relax your body – progressive relaxation is a good way. Tighten the muscles of each leg, then release. Then tighten and release the pelvic area. Continue with belly, chest, each arm, neck and head/face. Breathe deeply throughout.

Close your eyes and touch your tongue to the roof of your mouth. Invoke your soul to guide you in your practice. Feel yourself exactly as you are.

Is your overall feeling within of comfort and pleasure? Is it of tension? Do parts of you feel pained or shut down? Do any parts feel numb? Are there areas of physical pain? Just be aware of yourself exactly as you are – not as you think you could or should be.

Bring your attention into your heart and breathe deeply there. Invoke your own deepest love – the kind of love that you may more easily give to your dog, your cat, your children, God, or whoever or whatever it is easy for you to love. If you feel that it is not easy to love at all, simply be aware of this condition and love it unconditionally. Watch yourself from your Witness consciousness, simply observing what is and loving the exact way you are. Even love your seeming inability to love by being with the experience and not running away.

As you find any tight, painful or blocked areas breathe into them and radiate your love and compassion to them. Give those parts unconditional acceptance – not trying to fix them, ignore them, deny them or feel bad about them. Silently start chanting "Love melts all blockages" or "I love you" over and over as you bless your tight or dark areas with your breath and acceptance.

Continue for a minimum of 5 minutes, although 10 – 20 minutes or more will take you much deeper. You are tapping into the great healing power of pure awareness, breath and self-love.

You may have heard many times about meditating to open your heart, raise your consciousness, feel inner joy, move energy, etc. For this meditation don't worry about any of those ideals. This meditation is all about being with yourself just the way you are. Practice the essence of Billy Joel's famous song "I Love You Just the Way You Are" with yourself.

When you are done give thanks to your awareness and your heart.

There is a video on my website[63] called *Meditation on Mindfulness and Self Love* to guide you in this practice.

There is a simple and fun and powerful way to practice mindfulness while boosting your health and vitality. You do that by loving and acknowledging your internal organs. Why do this?

I'll tell you. Imagine that you got married to a partner who lived in the same house as you and slept in the same bed, but never spoke to you or even acknowledged your existence. You worked hard and steadily around the clock to serve and support him (or her). You knew that if you stopped serving him he would quickly die, but he just took it all for granted and never gave anything back to you.

He didn't even know where you were most of the time and did not care to learn! Not only that, but he sometimes made you sick by forcing you to eat toxic and harmful substances. You tried for decades to get his attention, to get him to acknowledge and love you but he persisted in abusing and ignoring you.

Finally in despair and a world of hurt, you collapsed and could serve your partner no more. Only then did he pay attention to you, and then only from a place of fear and panic. He rushed you to the hospital to try to save you. If the doctors were able to revive you and you recovered he soon went back to ignoring and abusing you again.

I'll bet that sounds like a really bad deal in a relationship, right?!?!?

Well that is how most of us treat our own internal organs! Go back and read the preceding paragraphs and see if you get what I am saying.

According to Traditional Chinese Medicine each of our internal organs has its own soul essence and consciousness. Each of the five major organs is the generator of one of our primary emotions, as follows:

> • *Anger* is generated by the liver and gall bladder, known as the Wood element
>
> • *Grief* is generated by the lungs and large intestine, known as the Metal element
>
> • *Worry* is generated by the spleen and stomach, known as the Earth element
>
> • *Joy, depression and anxiety* are generated by the heart and small intestine, known as the Fire element (there are two additional non-physical organs in the Fire element - the triple warmer and pericardium also involved with those emotions)
>
> • *Fear* is generated by the kidneys and urinary bladder, known as the Water element

As you can see, far from just being pieces of meat doing a bio-chemical function, our organs are vital parts of our personality, emotions and spirituality. Now does it make more sense to send love to them? A great way to do that is through this ancient Tao practice called the Inner Smile. This practice is similar to the self-love practice given above.

Practice 13-2: The Inner Smile

Here are the instructions:

- *Sit up straight in a relaxed position. Breathe deeply into your lower abdomen (Tan Tian).*

- *Think about the person, animal or place that most easily brings up feelings of love within you. Build that feeling of love, appreciation and gratitude.*

- *Now put a big smile on your face - yes a real physical smile. Tune into the love and appreciation behind your smile and amplify that feeling as much as you can.*

- *Visualize sending that big loving smile down into your own body (you can go back to loving your friend or animal very soon). Start by directing that smile into the center of your chest, into your heart. Put one of your hands over your heart to strengthen your focus there.*

- *Visualize your physical heart and heart chakra bathed in your own love and smile. See beautiful ruby red light surrounding and filling your heart and small intestine. Think about how tirelessly your heart has served you by keeping you alive through all kinds of ups*

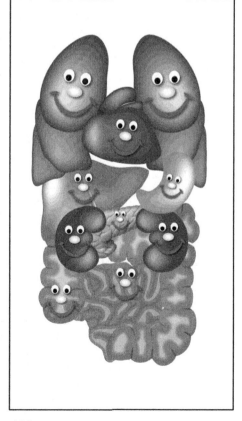

183

and downs, from the time you were formed in your mother's womb right up to the present moment. Give your heart love and gratitude.

▪ *When you feel complete with your heart, move your inner smile to your liver, under your right rib cage. Move your hand over your liver. Visualize beautiful healing green light surrounding and filling your liver and gall bladder. Think what an amazing servant your liver has been, keeping your alive and detoxifying all kinds of harmful substances you have taken in, and keeping your Ch'i, or vital energy flowing smoothly throughout your body.*

▪ *When you feel complete with your liver, move your inner smile to your spleen, under your left rib cage. Move one of your hands to be over your spleen. Visualize beautiful healing yellow gold light surrounding and filling your spleen, pancreas and stomach. Think what amazing servants your these organs have been, digesting your food, regulating your blood sugar and helping keep your immune system strong.*

▪ *When you feel complete with your spleen, move your inner smile to your lungs, in your chest. Move your hand to be over either one of your Lungs. Visualize beautiful healing white light surrounding and filling your lungs and large intestine. Think what an amazing servant your lungs have been, taking in air, filtering out toxins and keeping you alive.*

▪ *When you feel complete with your lungs, move your inner smile to your kidneys, in the upper part of your lower back. Move your hand to be over your kidneys if you can. Visualize beautiful healing blue or magenta light surrounding and filling your kidneys and bladder. Think what an amazing servant your kidneys have been, regulating body fluids, filtering blood, maintaining your healthy blood pressure and being a storehouse for deep energy reserves.*

You can also send love and your inner smile to other organs, such as your brain, uterus, thyroid, adrenals, or any painful parts of your body. This guided meditation is also on a video on my website[64].

[64] ibid

Love melts all blockages. Love is the greatest healer. When you love your organs you are loving yourself and taking a stand for Life. You are giving back to these tireless servants.

LET YOURSELF OFF THE HOOK – SELF FORGIVENESS

Back in Chapter 5 you read about some of the origins of the loose ends and unfinished business that swirls around inside our minds. Don Miguel Ruiz called this the "thousand voices speaking inside our heads". A lot of this is created by our past relationships that ended on a hurt, betrayed or angry note. Most of us have been through relationships of many kinds in our lives that ended in a negative or incomplete way. These could be intimate partners you parted with in anger or hurt, family members you felt hurt by and now avoid, bosses or business partners you have a judgment toward, or others. Depending on your age, that could be a lot of unfinished business and unresolved feelings.

If you believe that you have had multiple lifetimes that could total a dizzying amount of unfinished business! Each of those unresolved relationships could be draining some of your vital energy and clouding your heart. So it is a great idea to clean up the fog.

How? Mindfulness and self-love is a great way. The other main way is through forgiveness practice.

Whenever you feel hurt, rejected or other garden variety painful feelings it is a great opportunity to practice forgiveness. The most obvious form of forgiveness is to talk directly to a person you have had negativity with and apologize, or forgive them. If meeting with the person in person is too difficult, or if you can't talk to him because he is estranged or no longer living, you can still do a meaningful forgiveness practice by yourself.

The Hawaiian healing practice of *Ho'oponopono* consists of four simple phrases.

I am sorry
I forgive you
I love you
Thank you

Sincerely repeating these for 5 minutes or more can bring about beautiful emotional shifts. You can direct these words toward yourself, or a specific person you have had issues with. Or you can just say them to the Universe.

Many traumatized children blame themselves for their abuse. They have internalized a belief that the abuse happened because they were bad, or acted seductively with their perpetrator. Once they realize that these were false beliefs some deep self-blame may still linger, hard-coded into their body and subconscious mind.

Even if you have many yucky (shameful, painful, contracted, numb, etc.) feelings know that these are not really you. These are the reactions of your body to false beliefs and imprints you accepted into yourself[65]. Don't blame yourself for agreeing to take them in. You didn't know better when you did that. You were doing the best you could do at that time to try to deal with overwhelming experiences and survive.

You can only feel those yucky experiences in your body because the real you is pure consciousness. Come to know the difference between your true Self - your I AM presence - and these experiences. You can use the practices in *Chapter 10* to be present with the sensations in your body connected with these feelings.

Even if you were not abused you have felt the rigors of being alive. With all the blessings and joys available to us, being human can often be painful and challenging. We can easily blame ourselves for the ways life is hard for us – thinking things like "I'm so stupid because I keep making the same errors", "I hate that I keep getting depressed even after all this work on myself", "I can't

---

[65] See Chapter 5 for an inventory of the many forms of energetic imprints that can create "yucky" feelings

stand the way my body looks", "I haven't been able to fulfil my goals and get ahead financially yet so something must be wrong with me" and so on.

Having these kinds of critical and judgmental thoughts running in the background of your mind can drain your energy and lower the vibrational level of your consciousness. Not helpful!

We just have to accept that life is often full of bumps and bruises, and it is OK. Even big bruises. What is most important is to regularly take a few minutes to let yourself off the hook by practicing self-forgiveness.

Here is a short guided meditation on self-forgiveness. I recommend that you take the time to internalize this practice and do it regularly. Journal about any feelings or insights that come up as you do it. I recommend that you start by doing it sitting in a meditative state. As you internalize it you can do it as a walking meditation if you prefer.

Practice 13-3: Practice for Self-Forgiveness

1. Place the tip of your tongue on the roof of your mouth, behind your two front teeth. Start by taking three deep breaths into your lower abdomen, in through your nose and out through your mouth. Accentuate the outbreath.

2. Invoke the soul of Divine forgiveness – a part of the Divine. You may also invoke whatever spiritual being or source you feel most connected with, or the Universe. Take some deep breaths to acknowledge and welcome this presence into your space.

3. Create your intention to connect with any part of you that needs to be let off the hook. It is good to speak or think an intention statement like this: "It is my intention to connect with any parts of me, felt or hidden, that are holding any form of negativity, blame, shame, guilt, belief in failure or more. Please show me where you are in my body."

4. Feel into your body. Your body is a far more reliable witness than your mind. Feel for any areas that feel painful, blocked, stuffy, empty or any other form of discomfort. Let your attention be drawn to the primary body area that is connected to the experience or belief that needs to be transformed by forgiveness.

5. It is helpful to put a hand over this body area to help you focus on it.

6. Summon the sincere love of your heart and direct it to this body area. Feel your own love that you have given to everyone else go there. Bless that area by breathing deeply into it.

7. Offer yourself total forgiveness for any alleged mistakes you may have made that are connected with those painful or blocked areas of your body. The first time you do this practice just focus on self-forgiveness with self-talk like this:

"I forgive myself"

"I love you, I love you, I love you"

"Even though I have done (fill in the blank) or felt (fill in the blank) I totally love and accept myself."

It is valuable to combine energy tapping (*Chapter 11*) with forgiveness practice. Tapping on the acupressure points listed there as you make these statements can enhance your experience of forgiveness.

Once you feel a positive shift in letting yourself off the hook bring relationships with others into your practice. Offer apologies to those you have hurt, and forgiveness to those who have harmed you if you are ready to do so. Fill all your relationships with the golden light of forgiveness and love.

Continue with this for at least 5 minutes, so you can settle into the experience of forgiveness. Longer periods of forgiveness practice can take you deeper into resolution of emotional pain.

What is most powerful about this process is bringing the light of your consciousness to the blocked area. All the negative feelings about yourself thrive in unconsciousness. As you breathe deeply and focus on the area with love the unforgiven energy can transform. This can happen even if self-forgiveness has eluded you for a long time.

Sometimes you may feel overwhelmed by the extent of the forgiveness needed and you may need the support of a skilled healer or therapist. It is best to work with someone you trust and who can channel higher light while supporting you.

CONCLUSION

As you read above, self-love often seems to be the hardest form of love. If you have been through trauma you may encounter thoughts and feelings that could range from uncomfortable to terrifying as you quiet yourself and go within. This could reinforce beliefs in how unworthy, flawed or unlovable you are. This is where your love is so crucial. Simply persist in applying love and compassion to those parts of yourself. Love relentlessly.

One healer I know put it very well. She said that the hurting parts of us are like a scared child hiding under the staircase, refusing to talk or come out. Trying to coax the child to come out could be a frustrating experience, and just make his refusal to come out stronger. What works better is to consistently and frequently offer your love and compassion to the child, knowing that he will come out when he feels safe enough to do so. This takes patience with yourself. As that child part of you senses that you are not trying to get him to do anything, and are really loving him, he will start to feel safer. Then the changes and resolutions you are wanting will start to happen. That is the true miracle of love.

14

Unified Field Meditation

The heart is the integrator of all our organs and emotions

In each period of human history there have been new needs and new challenges. New technologies and solutions have sprung up to help meet those challenges at each of these stages. We are now in a unique time of expansion of consciousness on our planet. While this is ultimately a very positive evolution it has created its own set of challenges as governments, business and masses of people struggle to adapt to rapid changes.

New tools for harmonizing and enlightening our consciousness have emerged. One is the Unified Field Meditation.

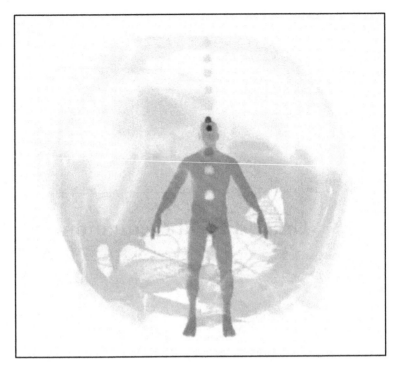

Unified field meditation

This is the simplest and quickest way to integrate your body and mind with the totality of your being. It expands your awareness of who you really are. And by expanded I don't mean spaced out. This meditation also grounds and energizes you for the joys and challenges of everyday life.

I unify my fields when I wake up in the morning, before most meals and as I prepare to work with clients. I also try to remember to be unified just about any other time as well.

Unified field theory has been a hot topic in physics since the early 1900's. Many physicists, including Einstein, have searched for a unified field theory that integrates all the known forces in the universe. Most scientists do not believe that a satisfactory unified theory has yet been proven. A growing number of physicists claim that what are called *superstring theories* may point to the existence of a unified field by demonstrating a common origin of electro-magnetism, gravity and nuclear forces[66].

In case you are not familiar with the term chakra, it refers to centers of energy and consciousness in our bodies. Those would be the spheres inside the man's body in the picture on the previous page.

People with PTSD, anxiety, chronic stress and just plain old everyday neurosis are not feeling a lot of integration within themselves. The Unified Field meditation puts all of your chakras, including the higher spiritual ones above your head, into alignment with each other and the love center of your Heart.

According to traditional Chinese Medicine our Heart is the center and integrator of all our organs and emotions. The Heart is called the Emperor in some acupuncture teachings. I am capitalizing the word Heart to refer to the love and energy center called the Heart Chakra more than just the physical heart organ. Yet both are included.

In the Unified Field meditation you will be guided to visualize a ball of golden light surrounding expanding levels of your chakra system. You can do the Unified Field meditation in 3 - 7 minutes. After you have practiced it for a while you can stay Unified all the time. As that happens the quality of your life will improve in many ways.

Below is a text version of this practice. You can also access a guided video version of the Unified Field meditation on my website. Once you have watched the video a few times you will be able to do the Unified Field meditation with your eyes closed, visualizing the expanding light ball. That is even more beneficial.

The expanding golden ball you will visualize as you do this practice is actually a torus, or toroidal shape. That is a sphere with cone-shaped indentations in the top and bottom of the sphere, with the narrow parts of each cone pointing toward each other in the

---

[66] http://strings.ph.qmul.ac.uk/engagement/brief-history-string-theory

center of the sphere. Electro-magnetic fields often take the shape of a torus.

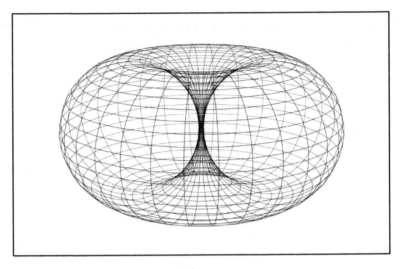

Torus

Practice 14-1: Unified Field Meditation

• *Visualize/imagine a luminous ball of light surrounding your physical body. This orb of light extends at least 5 feet above your head and about 4 feet below your feet and extends out all around you with your heart as its center. This field also penetrates and fills your body. This is your energy field, or energy bodies. This is your truest home, your place of one-ness and safety. You can consider this large orb of light to be the totality of your being.*

• *Breathe light coming from all parts of this field into your heart chakra, in the center of your chest. See a smaller golden light ball form within, through and around your heart center as a unified field of light. This light ball is shaped like a torus, with conical indentations in the top and bottom of the light ball shaped like whirlpools. The bottom whirlpool is inverted. Feel your heart relax and feel safe.*

• *Breathe light again from all directions into your heart chakra. Allow the golden ball around your heart to expand to encompass to the levels of your*

194

throat and solar plexus chakras as one unified field of light. Feel your whole chest area relax and let go and your breathing deepen.

▪ *Breathe light from all directions into your heart chakra and allow it to expand to encompass your brow and navel chakras as one unified field of light. Feel your nervous system relax and let down as it feels more and more at home.*

▪ *Breathe light from all directions into your heart chakra again and allow it to expand to encompass your crown and base chakras. Allow your physical body to vibrate faster as one unified field of light. Allow all the cells and DNA in your body to glow with golden light as they connect to your true Self.*

▪ *Breathe light from all directions into your heart chakra and allow it to expand, larger than your body, to encompass your 8th chakra, 8 inches above your head and below your base, as one unified field of light. Allowing your emotional body to know its own wholeness and completeness.*

▪ *Breathe light from all directions into your heart chakra and allow it to expand to encompass your 9th chakra, about 16 inches above your head and below your base, as one unified field of light. Allow your mental body to be a clear mirror of spirit.*

Breathe light from all directions into your heart chakra and allow it to expand to encompass your 10th chakra, about 24 inches above your head and below your base, as one unified field of light centered in spirit.

▪ *Breathe light from all directions into your heart chakra and allow it to expand to encompass your 11th chakra, about 32 inches above your head and below your base, as one unified field of light that knows its own divinity.*

▪ *Breathe light from all directions into your heart chakra and allow it to expand to encompass your 12th chakra, about 40 inches above your head and below your base, as one unified field of light. Allowing yourself to embrace and acknowledge your universal Self.*

- *Breathe light from all directions into your heart chakra and allow it to expand to encompass your 13th chakra, about 48 inches above your head and below your base, as one unified field of light. Allowing yourself to embrace and acknowledge the I AM presence that you truly are.*

- *Breathe light from all directions into your heart chakra and allow it to expand to encompass your 14th chakra, expanding infinitely around you, as one unified field of light. Knowing that I AM Source radiating through the totality of my being.*

- *I live within and through this Unified Field of Light. I AM this Unified Field of Light. As I interact with others, do my work, take care of my body and experience all of my human experiences I AM a Unified Field of Light.*

I cannot express in words the amazing value of practicing the Unified Field meditation. As you practice it faithfully the quality of your life experience will change. You will feel less scattered or fragmented. You will feel more and more connected to your core, and know that you are both human and Divine.

It is common for people to think of spiritual experience as something that mainly happens when they go to church, sit in silent meditation, visit sacred power spots on the Earth or go into an altered state. Practicing the Unified Field meditation will allow you to let go of those beliefs and to enjoy the knowledge that you are one with your divine source all the time. Some of my favorite times to enjoy being Unified are when I am stuck in traffic, trying to meet a challenging deadline or even while having a confronting argument with my partner. Even though parts of me are generally feeling stressed during such experiences it is awesome that a part of me can still feel my calm center and know that I am Unified with all the love and consciousness of the Universe. Sometimes I have to pinch myself and say wow.

Pretty groovy, eh?

PART III

GETTING HELP – NEW ACCELERATED METHODS FOR HEALING TRAUMA

If you want to find the secrets of the universe,
think in terms of energy, frequency and vibration
-- NIKOLA TESLA

Part II gave you valuable practices for healing yourself and reclaiming your calm center. Sometimes we also need support and guidance from others.

This section contains information about cutting edge treatment systems using vibrational medicine that have been recently developed. These systems can be remarkably effective for rapidly releasing trauma, clearing internal energy blockages and helping people free themselves so they can move forward on their inspired life path.

`

15

New Therapies for Rapid Release of Trauma

*Our "brain on trauma" is different than a healthy brain. In an attempt
to protect itself from perceived threats the brain often shuts down areas
that control our ability to have empathy, self-awareness, intimacy and more.*

It seems that nature often provides a remedy for every toxin in
the environment. For examples, exposure of the skin to poison ivy
or stinging nettles can produce painful, itchy rashes. Jewel weed,
which grows near poison ivy can reduce the pain and itching
caused by poison ivy. Horsetail, which grows near stinging nettles
relieves the pain of the nettles[67]. In the case of PTSD/trauma
both the problem and the remedy are based in the electrical-
energetic nature of the brain and nervous system.

As you probably know from media reports, our country has a big
problem with PTSD, or post-traumatic stress disorder. Thousands
of service people have returned from active duty complaining of
nightmares, traumatic flashbacks, headaches, insomnia and
depression. A high percentage of them have turned to drugs and

---

[67] http://www.explore-mag.com/Poisonous_Plants__Antidotes

alcohol for self-medication. These veterans are at high risk for being involved in domestic violence or suicide.

This problem is not restricted to veterans. Even higher numbers of people who have survived abusive childhoods, rape, automobile accidents and more suffer with PTSD.

There are still no reliable treatments for PTSD in current medical and psychological practice. A research study published in the *Journal of the American Medical Association* in 2015 reviewed 36 trials of psychotherapy treatments for PTSD over a 35 year period. The research showed that although some improvements were reported 2/3 of the people receiving the therapies still suffered with PTSD after the treatments[68]

Sounds discouraging, right?

Maybe, but an exciting new method has demonstrated remarkably rapid and effective results for permanently eradicating the suffering of PTSD. These methods have been shown to create long term relief of the flashbacks, crises and nightmares associated with past trauma within one clinical session. This system can be used as an adjunct to other psycho-therapeutic approaches to accelerate recovery.

This treatment method is in the realm of vibrational medicine. The word vibration refers to energy fields vibrating at various pulse rates, or frequencies. Vibrational medical practitioners apply specific frequencies of energy to the body for healing and therapeutic purposes. Various forms of vibrational therapies have been used going back thousands of years. These include light therapy, sound and music healing, flower essences, microcurrent therapy, homeopathy and even laying on of hands.

Vibrational medicine is having a major resurgence now through the use of modern electronics. It is being used to fill in gaps in our drug-based medical system. While western medicine offers dazzling life-saving interventions it usually deals poorly with

---

[68] Time Magazine, Aug 4, 2015 http://time.com/3982440/ptsd-veterans/

chronic pain and disease, and psycho-spiritual imbalances such as PTSD.

Before describing this new treatment method, here is a bit of background on the challenges of freeing people from old trauma.

PTSD is an increasingly common condition that robs people's peace of mind and in severe cases, even their ability to function. After profoundly traumatic experiences the alarm system of the brain (the amygdala) can get stuck on high alert. To some extent people with PTSD lose their ability to differentiate between true threats and harmless stimuli of life that are perceived as threats. In addition to the mental/emotional disorders listed above PTSD can also lead to a host of diseases linked with excess stress hormones being released in the body. Those diseases include heart disease, cancer, mental illness and auto-immune conditions.

Our "brain on trauma" is different than a healthy brain. In an attempt to protect itself from perceived threats the brain often shuts down areas that control our ability to have empathy, self-awareness, intimacy and more. (see *Chapter Two*).

THE PATHWAY OF PTSD

The terrifying experiences of PTSD are triggered when a person encounters something that reminds them of a past traumatic experience. Such experiences could be as innocent as being in a crowd of people or hearing a sudden loud noise, and are called triggers. When a person with PTSD experiences a trigger he is sensitive to it can start a lightning fast chain reaction. First the amygdala, the alarm center of the brain springs into action. It signals the nearby hypothalamus which is the link between the nervous system and endocrine gland systems of the body. The hypothalamus tells the anterior pituitary gland to release corticotropin-releasing hormone (CRH), which then triggers the adrenal glands to go into fight or flight mode and dump stress hormones into the bloodstream. See Chapter 2 for more details about PTSD.

Beyond the approximately 25 million people experiencing the debilitating effects of full blown PTSD in the USA I believe that there are many millions more that are dealing with what I call "low-grade PTSD". In fact that group may include most people in our culture. This modern epidemic of low-grade PTSD has been brought about by many influences that I have written about in Chapters 4 and 5.

Western medicine has very little to offer people suffering with PTSD except for palliative drugs which produce inconsistent results in controlling distressing symptoms. Such drugs may actually aggravate depression in people suffering with PTSD and often lead to increased risk of suicide. Thus the huge recent interest in finding more effective treatment methods.

HOW VIBRATIONS HEAL US

The forms of vibrational medicine showing the greatest promise for healing acceleration are color light therapy, sound healing and microcurrent therapies.

Light and color have been used for curative purposes since ancient times. Our human race grew and evolved surrounded by the colors of nature – blue sky and waters, green plants, red fire, brown earth, white snow, yellow sun and multi-color flowers, birds and insects. We not only take in color by seeing – our skin also has molecules called *cryptochromes* that absorb certain color wavelengths from the sun for supporting our health.

We exchange a great deal of energy and information with other people and the environment through our *chakra* system. Chakras are conscious tuned biologic transceivers in our bodies[69]. Each chakra vibrates at a rate supportive of the part of the body it is in. Each chakra outputs a characteristic color and responds instantly to the language of color.

---

[69] Chakras are transceivers because they receive vibrations from others and the environment, and also radiate their own state in the form of colors, emotions and information

The middle, emotional core of our brain is called the limbic area, and it governs our emotional responses. Our emotional responses are highly affected by color[70]. Artists and fashion designers know this well. It has been well documented that the color used to paint walls in prisons and mental health centers has had strong effects on the mental state of residents[71].

Each visible color is a code of information. When color light is applied to the body it could:

- Stimulate or relax one or more organs
- Stimulate or relax one or more endocrine glands, thus affecting hormonal balance
- Stimulate or relax one or more chakras
- Evoke an emotional response
- Shift the perception of pain

In general cool colors such as blue, indigo, violet and turquoise produce calming, grounding effects and can help relieve pain and inflammation. Warm colors such as red, orange, yellow and scarlet stimulate or excite the body or emotions. Green is right in the middle of the color spectrum, and was called "the great balancer" by Dinshah Ghadiali, one of the pioneers of medical color therapy.

In the PTSD healing system described here color light is usually combined with gentle electrical currents called *microcurrents*. Sound therapies are sometimes included.

Microcurrents are gentle electrical currents in the millionth of an amp range. Microcurrent therapy are very popular because using it has produced so many remarkable results for pain relief, wound healing and rejuvenation. There are also microcurrent frequency sequences that have been proven to help heal a host of diseases[72].

---

[70] http://www.arttherapyblog.com/online/color-psychology-psychologica-effects-of-colors/#.V__dFE0rKUk

[71] http://www.medicaldaily.com/pulse/color-psychology-why-prisons-started-painting-their-walls-bubblegum-pink-342312

[72] See the work of Carolyn McMakin for more on Frequency Specific Microcurrent: http://frequencyspecific.com/

In research studies microcurrent has been shown to speed up wound healing[73], strengthen tendons[74], boost energy production in cells[75], help heal macular degeneration of the eyes[76] and shrink some forms of cancerous tumors[77]. Few of these applications of microcurrent are in use by mainstream medicine yet, however.

Both microcurrent and color light therapies work on the principle of *energetic resonance*. This is the way vibrating energy fields affect each other. Each frequency of microcurrent and color of light resonate, or tune into specific parts and functions of the body. There are also many documented healing and balancing effects of sound healing and other vibrational therapies.[78]

HOW DO VIBRATIONAL ENERGIES HELP HEAL TRAUMA AND PTSD?

The answer to this question is multi-dimensional. Vibrational therapies tend to be empirical – that is they have been observed to work and so they are used. The theories of how they work are useful, but not complete. Here are some things we do know:

1. *Stimulation of acupuncture points has proven beneficial effects*. The science of acupuncture has been developed over thousands of years based on clinical observation of countless

---

[73] The Effects of Electric Current on ATP Generation, Protein Synthesis, and Membrane Transport in Rat Skin Clinical Orthopaedics and Related Research, #171, Nov/Dec. 1982

[74] Low-intensity Pulsed Galvanic Current and the Healing of Tenotomized Rat Achilles Tendons: Preliminary Report Using Load-to-Breaking Measurements Archives Physical Med Rehab, Vol. 68, July 1987

[75] See reference iv

[76] http://www.healingtheeye.com/microcurrent.html

[77] Nordenstrom, B. An Electrophysiologic View of Acupuncture: Role of Capacitive and Closed Circuit Currents and Their Clinical Effects in the Treatment of Cancer and Chronic Pain, American Journal of Acupuncture, Vol 17, #2, 1989

[78] You can read details on using microcurrent, color light and sound for emotional healing in my book Healing the Root of Pain available on www.microlightinstitute.com/products or through https://www.redwingbooks.com/

patients. Acupuncture points are small spots on meridians, or energy channels that can be stimulated with needles, heat, magnets or gentle electrical currents. Acupuncture is well-documented for promoting pain relief and healing of diseases. Each acupuncture point used on the body has a number on a meridian and a Chinese name.

The Chinese names of the acupuncture points describe its therapeutic function. Some of the points have names that indicate a physical function or location – such as *Jianyu* (Shoulder Bone) or *Hoku* (Meeting of the Valleys). Other acupuncture points have names that describe an emotional or spiritual quality. Some examples are *Shenmen* (Spirit Gate), *Yiji* (Wail of Grief) or *Tianzong* (Heavenly Ancestor).

Vibrational treatments for trauma use acupuncture points like these with strong healing effects on the spirit/soul level.

2. *Color light therapy can rapidly balance* chakras, emotions and hormonal secretions as described above.

3. *Microcurrent therapy has proven effects* for unblocking the energy meridians, promoting tissue healing and helping balance the brain and nervous system.

Another very powerful effect we have observed is how vibrational stimulation of acupuncture points can greatly amplify the benefits of psychological therapies. Millions of people have reduced anxiety using Emotional Freedom Technique (EFT) for self-treatment by tapping on acupuncture points[79]. Our experience shows that the benefits of these therapies seem to be supercharged when combined with simultaneous vibrational stimulation of acu-points.

I have developed a therapy system called Microlight therapy[80]. This is a combination of low-intensity microcurrent combined with color light therapy. Microlight therapy is used by healthcare

---

[79] See Chapter 11 for an introduction to energy tapping
[80] For more information on Microlight therapy email
support@microlightinstitute.com

and esthetic professionals for pain relief, rehabilitation, facial rejuvenation and non-needle acupuncture work.

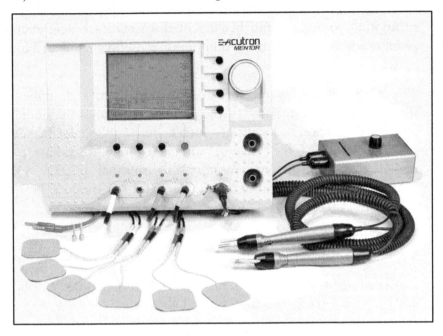

Acutron device developed by author

For over 25 years I led seminars throughout the world to train professionals in how to use microcurrent and light therapies for pain relief, weight loss, facial rejuvenation, pediatric treatment, post-stroke rehab and emotional healing (the subject of this chapter).

In my own healing practice I have specialized in helping people heal unresolved psychological issues so they can confidently move forward fulfilling their life purpose. Starting in the 1990's I started experimenting with ways to use vibrational therapies to accelerate that process. Eventually I developed an emotional healing system using Microlight therapy called Psycho-Neuro-Endocrine (PNE) Balancing. PNE Balancing involves applying microcurrent and light stimulation to the front and back of imbalanced body energy centers, or chakras. Clients are guided to visualize, tone or engage in healing dialogue while receiving the vibrational energy.

I have trained many acupuncturists and doctors in this system since then, and some have reported remarkable results for their clients. They have reported relief of depression and anxiety, healing bipolar disorder, release of eating disorders and improvements in dementia. One acupuncturist reported using PNE Balancing to save a few marriages by balancing the chakras of both partners when they were having serious relationship challenges.

There have been many gifted and creative practitioners who have worked with Microlight therapy in their clinical practices. Many of them have discovered new, innovative uses for it. One such practitioner is Dr. Greg Nevens, a clinical psychologist working in Portland, Maine. Nevens specializes in the treatment of trauma and chronic pain. He sees many veterans and civilians suffering with PTSD.

After purchasing the Acutron system Nevens experimented with using it to try to relieve these excruciating experiences. He discovered that stimulating certain acupuncture points with microcurrent and color light could interrupt the surge of traumatic energy in the brain associated with PTSD. It also appeared to short-circuit the associated release of stress hormones into the body. Using this knowledge he pioneered a remarkable PTSD healing system very an extraordinarily high success rate. I discovered similar effects in my own work with Microlight therapy on acupuncture points. An overview of our findings are presented below

THE DISCOVERY OF TERS

The PTSD treatment system developed by Nevens is called TERS, or *Traumatic Emotional Reintegration System*. Nevens applies Microlight stimulation to sets of bilateral acupuncture points on the arms or legs while a client visualizes a past traumatic episode in their mind. This system has demonstrated remarkable results for re-programming their brains to become less affected by traumatic memories.

According to Neven's research nightmares and traumatic flashbacks are associated with energy surges along the right side of the *corpus callosum*, the brain structure that connects the left and right hemispheres[81]. This energy surge seems to also be associated with the hormonal chain reaction that puts the body into a high stress fight or flight mode.

Veterans who had been suffering with incapacitating nightmares and flashbacks for decades have reported relief from these experiences after a single 25 minute TERS session.

Here are a few patient cases Nevens has used this method with:

1. *Vietnam Vet:* This man had had 5 – 7 flashbacks and nightmares a day for 45 years. He had 3 major traumatic memories that kept tormenting him. Nevens gave him one 25 minute session for each of the three traumatic memories, on different days. Four years after these treatments this veteran had not had one recurrence. This vet received a total of 3 TERS sessions and some follow up.

2. *Man who witnessed New York World Trade Center destruction in 2001:* On September 11 he heard the crash after the first plane hit, then after the second plane hit he saw people jumping out of building, with a white cloud of dust coming up the streets. After this he started having high anxiety, vigilance and mental dissociation which lasted for 13 years before being referred to Nevens for treatment. By this time he was in his early 30's. This patient received one 25 minute TERS session. After this single treatment he stopped having the high anxiety, nightmares and flashbacks. Only after these experiences were gone he realized that he had become used to them as his norm.

---

[81] For backup on this see B Engdahl, et al., "Post-traumatic stress disorder: a right temporal lobe syndrome?", J. Neural Eng. 7, 2010)

3. Woman who got pregnant as teenager: She was originally referred to Nevens for treatment of fibromyalgia pain when she was 60 years old. After a few treatments her pain was relieved and she was able to stop taking 90% of her medications. During her later sessions in this series she told Nevens about issues with vaginismus and painful intercourse that had bothered her for over 20 years. As a result of these conditions she had not been able to be intimate with her husband. She had also gone through 5 – 6 female operations for issues including vaginal prolapse and uterine bleeding. She believed that all of this was associated with a traumatic experience from her youth.

As a teenager she had learned she was pregnant and told her mother about it, who then told the father. The parents sent the girl to England for an abortion in an atmosphere of shame. The abortion was done in a horrendous way with massive bleeding on the floor and the fetus thrown into in a trash can.

This woman received one TERS treatment to release the trauma from her teenage abortion. Soon after this single session she was able to be sexually intimate with her husband for the first time in 20 years, with no pain at all.

Nevens has also used TERS successfully for rape victims and people who have been through car accidents and near death experiences. What is most remarkable is that over his hundreds of cases over the last 8 – 10 years he can only remember two patients who did not have a positive response to this vibrational therapy. He believes that people with brain injuries may not respond well to it, and that could be the reason for those two non-responses.

MY EXPERIENCES WITH RELIEVING TRAUMA AND PHOBIAS

Phobias are irrational fears that cause people to avoid certain experiences. Phobias usually develop in response to a past traumatic experience with the object of the phobia. In other words, a child who was bitten and injured by a big dog could develop a phobia of dogs after that. As part of my work with healing trauma I have experimented with Microlight therapy for helping clear phobias.

I have used the TERS method with clients who had phobias preventing them from speaking in front of a group, walking in high places, driving through big cities, gardening, snakes, having their body touched and more. In most cases these people have been able to do those activities without fear after receiving one or two treatment sessions. Some clients who had chronic pain associated with old trauma have felt relief for the first time in many years after 1 - 3 of these sessions.

As an example, I met a 53 year old massage therapist named Susan (name changed) in New Jersey who had a severe phobia of her feet being touched. As a child Susan had stepped on a rusty nail. After being rushed to the hospital she was treated brutally by some doctors who held her down while the nail was dug out of her foot without adequate anesthesia. This experience deeply traumatized Susan, and she could not bear to have anyone touch her feet after that. It was even hard for her to touch her own feet, and was an ordeal for her to put socks on and off.

I started by asking her to rate her phobia by choosing a number between 1 and 10. 10 represented extreme aversion to having her feet touched, and 1 was no aversion. Susan said that her phobia was off the chart above 10. I then used the Acutron to treat three sets of acupuncture points on her wrists, ankles and back of her neck. With each point, one wand was put on the right side and one on the left side. While doing this I asked her to visualize first the traumatic hospital experience and then a person touching her feet as an adult.

After about ten minutes of this therapy I asked Susan to rate her phobia again. She told me she was not sure about what the new score was, so I asked her if I could have permission to touch her feet gently. With great reluctance she said I could try it. It touched one of her feet gently. She did not react, so I touched more firmly. There was still no reaction. Then I asked if I could massage her feet. She nodded her head and I massaged her feet firmly for a few minutes. Susan was looking at me with amazement because she was not feeling discomfort about her feet being massaged. After follow up I found that this relief of the phobia lasted for at least a few months. I was unable to give her a follow up treatment due to geographic distance.

Another case was an acupuncturist named Sean who had been assaulted while driving through a big city. After that experience he avoided driving through San Francisco, which he lived near. This was causing him a lot of challenges and stress because he needed to drive frequently in the area. After Sean received one phobia release session from me I did not hear from him for over a year. After that time he wrote me an email telling me that ever since that single treatment he had been able to drive through San Francisco without much difficulty, and he was very grateful.

SUMMARY

There is a modern epidemic of people whose lives have been adversely affected by past trauma. These effects range from feelings of blockage and fear about life to being incapacitated by PTSD. Psychotropic drugs and psycho-therapeutic methods have only been able to help people with these issues to a limited extent. Some innovative psychological methods such as EMDR (rapid eye movement), Emotional Freedom Technique and cognitive therapies have shown greater promise[82] These methods, however have not provided consistent results for most people with severe trauma.

When microcurrent, color light or sound vibrational therapies are applied to acupuncture points and chakras with strong effects on emotions and consciousness, and this is combined with skilled conscious guidance by a qualified practitioner, results have been far better. The methods of TERS and PNE Balancing have demonstrated immediate, long-lasting and much more consistent results.

[82] See Chapter 11 for details on energy tapping and EMDR

Note – contact information for practitioners of these systems can be found in Appendix 2 section at the end of this book.

16

Biofield Healing

Biofield healing does not focus on fixing problems. It focuses instead on re-awakening and re-connecting our bodies and minds to our true Self where the problems don't exist

In my work with chronic pain and trauma patients over the last 34 years I have studied and worked with many therapeutic systems, always trying to discover ways to give my clients the best possible results. After all this experience I have concluded that the most effective system for treating people with PTSD, chronic pain or self-sabotaging emotional blocks is a combination of vibrational energy therapies, intuitive counseling and Biofield therapies.

Vibrational therapies include use of sound waves, color light or microcurrent (low-level electrical currents) as written about in the previous chapter. These therapies require electronic equipment that generates specific frequencies. Biofield healing, on the other hand, does not require any equipment.

The biofield is the field of living, conscious energy that surrounds and permeates all living things. The term was originated in 1992 at a National Institutes of Health meeting. The biofield of the body consists of measureable electrical fields generated by the brain,

217

heart, nervous system and cellular activity. There are also subtle energies contributing to the field that cannot yet be directly measured by test equipment, but can be verified through other, indirect methods such as hand sensing and kinesiology (muscle testing).

Biofield healing is a system for facilitating rapid and positive psychic shifts in people through clearing and adjusting of their biofield. Using a combination of vibrational therapies and biofield healing I have helped clients release chronic pain, relieve long-term phobias, improve sleep, boost energy levels, get clear mentally and significantly reduce anxiety and depression. Beyond relieving distress, this method can also help people clear blockages to success in their career or personal relationships.

Biofield healing can also be a great support for people on a path of spiritual awakening and ascension, as it helps remove feelings of disconnection. Many people receiving sessions describe tangible experiences of their one-ness with spiritual source.

The method that works in all these cases is the transmission of higher spiritual light into dark or disconnected areas of the biofield. Through a course of treatments people learn to find and tune into their own inner calm center, and stop escalating fearful and stress-based thoughts. This frees them up to move forward creating a purposeful, inspired life.

Let's start with a few recent examples of Biofield healing from my own practice.

A young woman named Evelina (name changed) recently met me at a medical conference I was presenting at. She told me about the anxiety she had been feeling after coming to this country. Instability in her living situation combined with fallout from a past traumatic relationship had been causing her to have nightmares and fear of going out by herself in public. After our discussion Evelina started receiving a series of remote Biofield Healing sessions. These were truly remote because she was living on the East Coast and my office is near San Francisco, over 3000 miles apart.

A few days after her first Biofield session Evelina spoke with me on the phone and told me that she had gone out by herself to take care of errands with much less apprehension. She had also had a dream at night in which she fearlessly fought and triumphed over a snake, a creature she had been terrified of throughout her life. She felt more confident after these experiences, and she continued to gain confidence and inner calm over a series of sessions.

I worked with another woman named Chrissy from upstate New York who had been dealing with chronic back pain. After two remote Biofield sessions her back pain was gone. That was certainly a positive outcome, yet another side effect of the treatments was even more interesting.

Chrissy was single and lived in a small town. There was an ex-boyfriend in the town that she kept running into, and this had been painful for her. Seeing him pushed her emotional buttons each time and threw her off balance. The way he acted with her kept bringing old hurts back up to the surface, like they had just happened. Chrissy was furious with herself for being so vulnerable to this man, but was unable to change this pattern. Soon after her second Biofield sessions she ran into this man again. This time felt detached and unperturbed – with no feeling of buttons being pushed.

Many doctors would find it hard to believe that results like these could happen so quickly, and over such a long distance. Yet people that I and other remote healers work with report experiences like this regularly.

One of my recent local clients was a man named Eduardo who was estranged from his female partner. Due to his heavy drinking and frequent criticisms she asked him to move out of their home. Eduardo came to me complaining about frequent anxiety, depression and fear of losing his tech job in Silicon Valley. After he completed a month of Biofield sessions Eduardo went on a trip, and I did not hear from him again for a couple of months. When we finally touched base again he told me that he was no longer drinking, anxiety was no longer bothering him and he had a great new job. Perhaps best of all, his partner had taken him back and they were now doing very well together.

Before describing more about what Biofield Healing is and how it works I will put it in the context of more familiar medical systems.

All physical things, including our bodies and our world can be described in three dimensions (length, width and height). Therefore we can call modern Western medicine a three dimensional (3D) healing system since it primarily works on what is physical and bio-chemical.

Complimentary and alternative healing arts such as acupuncture, chiropractic, homeopathy, naturopathy and more have become very popular because they help to fill in the gaps left by Western medicine. To varying degrees these systems work with the inter-relatedness of the body and mind, and our relationship with the cycles of nature. Physics calls time the fourth dimension. By acknowledging time we can better understand the deeper root causes of our pain and diseases. Therefore these alternative, holistic therapies can be referred to as fourth dimensional (4D) healing systems.

I consider Biofield healing to be a fifth dimensional, or 5D healing art. What does this mean? It means that Biofield healing does not focus on fixing problems. It focuses instead on re-awakening and re-connecting us to our true Self where the problems don't exist. It does this through re-establishing the tangible experience of the Self through the body. So many people have lost much of this direct awareness of spiritual source through the body due to past trauma, fear and social conditioning.

The fifth dimension is the aspect of our consciousness that has never been hurt, wounded or diseased, and has always been with us, running in the background of our minds. Biofield healing reconnects our bodies and minds to this healthy and complete core part of ourselves. It is a much more effective and rapid healing method than trying to fix problems, which can sometimes feel like a losing battle!

THE SCIENTIFIC BASIS OF BIOFIELD HEALING

The human biofield surrounds and permeates the physical body. Our human biofields interact with the energy fields of other people around us and the Earth. In terms of physics, that makes us an *"open system"* – one that interacts and exchanges energy with its environment. This is why you can feel drained after being around people who are negative or needy "energy vampires". On the more positive side, it is also why we love being around people who are loving and positive.

Our biofield is also strongly affected by man-made electro-magnetic fields, usually with negative effects on our health and well-being. One likely reason for the spike in stress-related pain and disease is that most people live in urban areas removed from the harmonious energies of nature, surrounded by these more stress-inducing fields.

People suffering with anxiety, inflammation, pain, disease and emotional trauma will have disturbances in areas of their biofield. A skilled practitioner can perceive these as dark areas, holes or distortions in the biofield. They can help resolve the root causes of pain and trauma by adjusting the energy fields in conjunction with intuitive counseling.

In many cases adjustments to a person's energy biofield are more important for freeing people from pain and disease than treatments done directly on the physical body. In any case biofield healing can augment and support effectiveness of physically-based treatment systems including western medicine, psychology, massage, acupuncture, physical therapy and much more. I personally had a 30 year career as an acupuncturist and energy medicine practitioner, and was able to help large numbers of people using these arts. The reason I focus on Biofield healing in my practice now is that that the beneficial changes my clients report are much more on the core level of their experience.

Healing arts that work with subtle energy fields have long been seen as separate from scientific medicine. This has been changing in recent years. There is now growing recognition of the energetic nature of life through many hundreds of recent studies. This is opening up exciting new avenues for more effective treatments for chronic pain, trauma, PTSD and hard-to-treat diseases.

This quote from bio-physicist Beverly Rubik clearly states the basis for energy medicine:

> *Living systems may be regarded as complex, nonlinear, dynamic, self-organizing systems of energetic and field phenomena. At the highest level of organization, each life form may possess an innate biologic field, or biofield, a complex, dynamic, weak energy field involved in maintaining the integrity of the whole organism, regulating its physiologic and biochemical responses, and integral to development, healing, and regeneration (Rubik, 1993, 1997, 2002b).*[83]

A retrospective research study published in 2010 reviewed 66 clinical studies using a variety of biofield therapies in different patient populations [84]. The conclusion of the study was that biofield therapies show strong positive evidence for reducing pain among chronic pain patients, and moderate evidence for reducing cancer pain, negative behavioral symptoms and anxiety among hospitalized patients. While this is a good validation for the efficacy of biofield healing methods, I believe that there are methods now available that are more powerfully effective than those examined in this study.

WHAT HAPPENS IN A BIOFIELD SESSION?

During Biofield healing sessions the client usually lies face up on a treatment table in a meditative space. The biofield healer uses his or her hands and intuitive sensing abilities to feel for areas of the client's energy fields that requires clearing or balancing. Healing light is then directed into the client's energy fields (non touch), or into energy lines and points on the client's body (with gentle

---

83 http://www.faim.org/measurement-of-the-human-biofield-and-other-energetic-instruments
84 International Journal of Behavioral Medicine, March 2010, Volume 17, Issue 1, pp 1–16

touch). These could be described as forms of spiritual energy acupuncture where no needles are required.

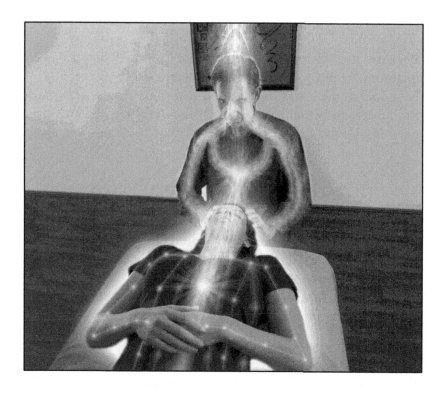

An attuned Biofield healer can sense where the subtle energy wiring of client's bodies are frayed or broken, and can help restore them to full connection and function over a series of sessions. Broken energy connections may manifest through feelings of depression, emptiness, fatigue or loss of life direction. Sessions may also include the removal of interfering energies from the body. In energy healer terminology these are often called *"energy implants"*. Similar to the concept of samskaras introduced in *Chapter 6*, implants are analogous to buggy computer viruses, and can block and divert people from their well-being and success.

Almost everyone who receives biofield healing experiences a deep sense of relaxation and well-being. Those that are more sensitive to energy usually also report blissful feelings of energy and light moving through their bodies. Some other common experiences reported by clients include changes in their breathing, resurfacing of past memories, waves of emotion, release of pain or feelings of being "lightened up".

Because the energy directed through Biofield healing is in the quantum realm geographical distance does not matter. The benefits are the same whether the receiver is in the same room as the healer, or around the world. Many clients prefer to have in-person sessions, but it is not necessary.

HOW DOES BIOFIELD HEALING WORK?

Acupuncturists work with energy pathways in the body called meridians. Meridians contain acupuncture points which can be stimulated with needles, heat or microcurrent for relief of pain and healing of diseases. The key understanding is that these meridians inter-connect the surface of the body with internal organs, and connect the organs with all aspects of our mind and emotions.

According to many metaphysical systems the Earth also has its own meridians, also called ley lines. These are pathways of energy flow that have greater abundance of magnetism and vital energy. The Earth meridians have frequently become major highways, shipping lanes or animal migratory pathways. Areas rich in ley lines are often recognized as sacred sites for pilgrimage and building of temples and cathedrals.

There are also thought to be meridians inter-connecting our Earth with the solar system, galaxies and the Universe. These are also described as inter-connecting lines of energy [85]. They are considered to be holographic because the meridian lines in the human body reflect the meridians of the Earth and cosmos.

---

[85] Examples are https://www.anasatara.org/sacred-energy-sites/what-is-a-ley-line or http://www.bibliotecapleyades.net/ciencia/antigravityworldgrid/ciencia_antigravit yworldgrid06.htm

By this belief the meridians of human beings were in more active, conscious connection and flow with these Universal lines of force at one time, and life was very different. Through what has often been called the "fall from grace" our race largely disconnected our body's energy pathways from those of the Universe. This led to all manner of pain, disease, conflict, scarcity and spiritual disconnection.

The root of most, if not all, pain, depression, fatigue and disease is a deep sense of disconnection from our loving, abundant true Self. As you get physically re-wired through Biofield healing and your own meditation practice you move out of separation and into the love and joy of living fully. Your energies are freed up from struggle for creative self-expression and giving your greatest gift to the world.

We might say that Biofield healing helps reverse our fall from grace, putting us back into direct connection with universal energy and consciousness. Now, that's something to get excited about!

As you are reconnected the innate wisdom of your body can much more readily restore and rejuvenate itself. No claims or promises of specific medical results can be made for Biofield healing, yet relief of pain and improvements in health and well-being are common. These changes may be noticed right away or several days later.

The ultimate goal of this work is not just alleviation of distressing symptoms. It is to bring people into a clear and grounded consciousness where they can make new, life-affirming choices and move forward with creating a meaningful and fulfilling life.

IV

WHERE TO GO FROM HERE

All the answers lie within you. Now your job
is to match them up with all the questions.
-- STEVE BHAERMAN ("SWAMI BEYONDANANDA")

This section contains one chapter and three appendices:

17

Community and Giving Back

Our own self-realization is the greatest service we can render the world
-- RAMANA MAHARSHI

If you have read this far, congratulations! You are well on your path of fulfillment and awakening just by being you.

I hope this short book has served to inform you about why you may have been experiencing some of the strange or difficult things you have been going through, and inspire you to take a bold stand to reclaim your calm center. In our modern society that is one of the greatest treasures we can lay claim to.

Reclaiming your sacred inner core is not a one shot deal. It is an ongoing commitment to living a conscious, juicy life full of meaning and contribution.

I have figured out for myself that maintaining my calm center is the most important action on my to-do list. Or should it be my "to-be" list?!? The quality of everything to do with my professional work, relationships, finances, health, achievements and spirituality is totally based in this. All these areas of my life, and your life,

231

work better and flow more beautifully when we are connected to our inner garden of tranquility.

Reclaiming your calm center is a revolutionary political act as well. A top way to make a difference to your country and world is to be determined to stay in your calm center as much as you can. From that place make a commitment to share and radiate love. All you need to do is be yourself, love yourself and be mindful in the present moment. Love whatever arises – that which seems good and that which seems difficult and challenging. Love melts all blockages. As you live more in the now moment you may be led to take political action or do acts of service. When you are staying connected with your calm center these actions will come less from polarization – "us against them" - and more because you are already part of the solution.

As you learn to live from your calm center an urge often arises to be with other people who are also claiming and enjoying their calm center. This is called spiritual community. This is a hot subject here in my area. There is a growing hunger for opportunities to get together with others who value sharing love, music, spiritual practices, healing, education, childcare and conscious businesses. Creating and participating in spiritual community is a great way to make a difference on our planet, as the power of groups amplifies our positive sphere of influence.

As Marianne Williamson's quote so eloquently stated, we are far more powerful than we know. People joke about those who want to change the world because it may seem so "pie in the sky", "woo-woo" or other derogatory terms. The truth is that you do have the power to change the world! It starts with transforming your inner world and then it radiates outward. The Unified Field and anapana meditations are particularly powerful ways to do and be that.

Listen to and believe the small still voice in your heart. Have the courage to believe in your visions and dreams, and take action to make them your reality. We are all being tested and challenged during this time of transition on our planet. Our life issues and psychological imbalances are not truly problems - they are our gateway into an expanded life. These are the precise areas where our steadfast love, faith and mindfulness can create demonstrations of the power of healing and renewal. These will uplift your life and be an inspiration to others.

Once you are getting more grounded in your own inner core you will tend to feel your heart opening more. It is a natural tendency to want to give back and share some of your own treasure of love and peace with others.

This is the ecological way of nature. Everything and everybody serves the greater good. Trees serve by producing fruits or nuts, shade, home for birds and animals, oxygen and when cut down it provides wood. Each plant and animal has its own balanced place within the eco-system that helps maintain the network of life (except when humans meddle in it).

In his book *The Prophet*, Kahlil Gibran beautifully describes people who give of themselves unconditionally in the same way that nature does:

And there are those who give and know not pain in giving, nor do they seek
joy, nor give with mindfulness of virtue;
They give as in yonder valley the myrtle breathes its fragrance into space.
Through the hands of such as these God speaks, and from behind their eyes.
He smiles upon the earth.

I've always loved this quote because it expresses how it is our true nature to serve.

Serving others is probably the most powerfully effective way to bless your own healing journey. That is because what goes around comes around. That which you give to others blesses you.

If you are in the early stages of recovery from trauma just coping with life and dealing with your own healing process will likely consume most of your emotional bandwidth. As you reclaim your calm center and ground more with your true Self you will have more to give to others. Yet at any point on your healing journey you can love and serve.

The master healers I have studied with taught that we serve through being who we are. We serve by going through our own healing and learning process because we are laying tracks in the wilderness that others can follow more easily.

Giving back can take many forms. I will list below 16 powerful ways you can be of service. Consider putting into action any of these that speak to you:

1. Get in touch with what you are most passionate about and courageously choose to do that thing, in spite of any obstacles or challenges. When you are doing what you are most passionate about you will serve in the most effective and expansive way.

2. Commit to your daily consciousness practice, using the practices in Section II of this book or others. Develop the self-love and self-discipline to prioritize doing your practices consistently. Remember, even doing 5 minutes of any of these practices twice a day could rock your world! As you do this and gain the benefits your life will bless people around you in many amazing and unforeseen ways. Your friends and family members have their psychic antennas up, and can sense when there is a real change in you. When they intuit that you are doing this it will affect them[86].

3. Come into your body awareness as often as possible. Whenever you are aware of your body you are in the Now moment. You will be more likely to notice others, share love and radiate your light when you are present.

4. Smile at strangers and befriend lonely or hurting people.

5. Volunteer for a local cause you believe in. Take a stand. Be an active part of the solution. The opportunities to do this and make

[86] If your friends or family members are invested in fear and negativity your commitment spiritual practice could also draw further negativity or criticism from them. This is again an opportunity for you to practice consciousness. As hard as it may be, intend to love them unconditionally and not react to their negativity. If you need more space from negative friends or family members do your best to give that to yourself.

an impact have greatly expanded since the 2016 Presidential election.

6. Resolve to be extra loving and understanding to the people in your life – especially when it doesn't come easy.

7. Know you are a source of blessings and share them often. Whenever you arrive in a new place such as a class, a concert, your workplace, a crowded train or a sports event take a moment to pray for all the people and animals there and ask the Divine to offer them a blessing. It is good to surround yourself with white light of protection before doing this if you have experienced taking on energy from others. Always offer your blessings by saying *"please give an appropriate blessing for the greatest good"*. This covers all your bases and will keep you safe and in integrity.

8. Help create spiritual community in any way you can. This could include organizing a meetup group [87], participating in online forums or just having a few conscious friends over regularly. There is a real hunger for more of this in our society.

9. Practice radical forgiveness for yourself and others. This is one of the most powerful healers, and is always available to you. (see *Chapter 13*)

10. Help champion and protect the Earth. Donate to or work with environmental groups you resonate with.

11. Become a healer if you are guided in that direction. This can take many forms including learning to offer healing touch to family members, participating in group healings for humanity or expanding your abilities if you are already a doctor or health care practitioner[88]. This is a major growth industry now!

---

87 www.meetup.com You can join and create your own group of interest, and meetup will promote it to people in your area with interest in your kind of group
88 I offer training and mentorship to doctors and healers in expanding their healing abilities. See www.bridgetomastery.com

12. Learn to hear and obey the small still voice of higher guidance within you. This gets easier to do as you reclaim your calm center. You can be sure that you are serving when you are obeying your own higher guidance.

13. Use your creative abilities to share truth and joy. This could take the form of blogging, writing a book or poetry, composing music, dancing, acting or more. Ask your higher Self to bring a higher level of consciousness through your creations so they serve on a higher level.

14. Take care of yourself. Take the time to exercise, relax, meditate and sleep. Only put healthy things into your body. Spend time with people you love. As they say on the airlines "Fasten your own air mask first, then help the person next to you". You can serve much more effectively when you are taking care of yourself well.

15. See and affirm your one-ness with all life.

16. Resolve to stay consciously connected with your calm center. All the things listed above will flow much more naturally and joyfully when you are making this a priority.

17. Get intimate with nature, God's great creation, to learn more about beauty, grace, abundance and the inter-relationship of beings.

I was at a magnificent concert this year called Songs for All Beings. One thing I heard there that resonated with me was that none of us fully heal by ourselves. Yes, we can greatly improve the quality of our lives through the methods presented in this book and other sources. But as long as there are suffering people and animals on our planet we will never be fully healed. That is because we are all inter-connected, and at the deepest core we are One.

Most of what has been presented in this book are insights and methods for personal healing. This has got to be our first step in recovery. If you are not committed to loving and honoring yourself the ultimate benefits of any service you offer will be limited and can even contribute to the problem. When you are touching into your calm center, regardless of how imperfectly you think you are doing so, your presence brings light into the situations you show up in. That is the service most needed on this planet now. Hold the space of One-ness within the calm center of your breath, make sure you are in love, and then take action. Your contributions will then have ripples far beyond what you would imagine.

APPENDIX 1

Explanation of Terms Used in This Book

There are my definitions of terms that are from languages other than English, are metaphysical or require some explanation.

- **3rd dimension (3D)** – the physical level of reality. In consciousness 3rd dimensional reality is dominated by the left, logical brain and is focused into physicality and denial of spirituality. 3D is characterized by the limitations of matter, thereby often resulting in conflict and scarcity. Western medicine is based in 3D consciousness.

- **4th dimension (4D)** – the physical level of reality plus the dimension of time. Most metaphysics exist within the 3rd and 4th dimensions. While valuable and fascinating to understand 4D is still based in dualities of good/bad, light/dark, high/low, etc. Holistic healing systems are based in a combination of 3D and 4D consciousness.

- **5th dimension (5D)** – the realm of unlimited possibilities that is based on unity and one-ness. Biofield healing and other systems that awaken people to their true Self are based at least partially in 5D.

239

- **Agreements** – Voluntary choices sovereign beings make that create a commitment or limitation of some kind on themselves. Most of us have made multiple agreements that have given our power away in numerous ways.

- **Amygdala** – Small bodies in the central brain that when triggered put the body into a state of reaction and defense based on stored memories of past traumas.

- **Anapana** – A primary meditation practice taught by the Buddha that is based on following the breath with the mind.

- **Annicha** – Impermanence of all material and mental things and experiences. It is the recognition of annicha that motivates people to practice the universal path of consciousness.

- **Biofield** – The field of conscious energy surrounding and permeating our physical bodies.

- **Biofield healing** – A system in which transmissions of spiritual light are directed into a person's biofield to help heal disconnections or blockages or help remove negative influences, so that the person can be freed up to live a fulfilling life free of pain and limitation.

- **Buddha** – Means "enlightened one" in Pali. Any of us can be a Buddha.

- **Calm center** – the still point within you that is always present, even when you are feeling discombobulated. The art of meditation is learning to tune into your calm center no matter what is going on around you or even within your own mind.

- **Chakras** – Spinning energy centers in the body that regulate our organs, glands, emotions and aspects of our consciousness. There are seven major chakras in the body as well as additional chakras below and above our physical body that connect us with the Earth and higher levels of Self. Chakra means "wheel" in Sanskrit.

• **Curse** – a software program placed into the sub-conscious mind of another person that is designed to create painful, fearful or limiting experiences.

• **Dharma or Dhamma** – Your true path that in accord with the laws of the Universe.

• **Discombobulation** – A scattered condition of the mind that affects most modern people, in which it is hard to relax and concentrate on what is real and brings you peace and joy.

• **EFT** – Emotional Freedom Technique, a system of self-healing in which people tap acupuncture points on their own bodies with their fingertips while repeating affirmations or other healing statements.

• **EMDR** – Using rapid eye movements for psycho-therapy and release of trauma.

• **Enlightenment** – A state of knowing and experiencing your true Self in your body.

• **Equanimity** – The quality of being content within yourself and avoiding entangling reactions to experiences and sensations.

• **I Am presence** – The true Self in expression as the higher consciousness part of an individual.

• **Karma** – Action, and the law that "what goes around comes around". The law of karma states that each of us tastes the fruits of our positive and negative actions through our own experiences.

• **Implant** – A limiting or sabotaging program installed into a person's mind or body, designed to take away their sovereignty.

The person receiving the implant must agree on some level to accept it, and this often happens in non-conscious ways.

• **Limbic system** – The middle, emotional center of the brain. It includes the amygdala, hippocampus, thalamus, hypothalamus, basal ganglia, and cingulate gyrus.

• **Matrix, the** – The name of a hit movie. This movie very well illustrated the truth that the "world" we believe we live in is not necessarily what is most real. I like to use the term *"the matrix"* to refer to the web of illusion propagated through the medias and belief systems of the human race that tries to keep us from knowing who we are as sovereign beings.

• **Meditation** – The practice of focusing concentration within oneself. The most valuable forms of meditation are those that require no outside input such as audio recordings, music, guided meditations, imagery, mantras or diagrams to look at. They consist of the practice of concentrating on what is already happening inside your body, especially the breath and bodily sensations.

• **Meridians** – pathways of vital energy flow in the body, the Earth and the Universe

• **Microcurrents** – Electrical currents in the millionth of an amp level. Therapies using microcurrent are very effective for pain relief, tissue healing acceleration, rejuvenation, emotional balancing and much more.

• **Mindfulness** – The practice of viewing life from the perspective of your Witness consciousness, so your reactions are lessened and you gain greater equanimity of mind.

• **Mitote** – A Toltec term that means "fog". Don Miguel Ruiz referred to the discombobulated condition of the human mind as a mitote in his book *The Four Agreements.*

• **Monkey mind** – A description of the overactive activity in the mind that keep most people tense, off balance and having difficulty concentrating and experiencing inner peace.

• **Oversoul** – This word comes from a metaphysical perspective that each of us is an individual soul that is part of a larger being that could be called a soul family. When you meet people you have a powerful resonance with they could be expressions of your soul family. Monad is another term for this. The Oversoul and other related ideas appear in the published works of Alice Bailey.

• **Pain body** – Characteristic forms of emotional pain that are shared among groups of people with some shared affinity. For example, there are pain bodies for all women, all men, all Jews, all Muslims, all Russians, all gay people, etc.

• **PTSD** – Post Traumatic Stress Disorder. A huge epidemic in our society.

• **Qi** – Life force energy in the body that has a quality of consciousness

• **Samskara or Sankara** – Deep conditioning of our sub-conscious mind that is a major cause of suffering. I have called this "mental gunk" in this book. We create Samskara by the habit of reacting to the sensations of life by either craving them or having aversion for them. The best cure for Samskara is developing equanimity of mind through meditation and service to others.

• **Self** – Who we really are beyond the illusions and limitations of our minds. The true Self, higher self, divine self, God within.

• **Shaman** – A person adept in accessing alternate states of consciousness and promoting healing and expansion of awareness in others.

• **Siddhi** – Special powers developed by yogis after exercising intense concentration over long periods of time.

• **Soul standing** – The level of empowerment a person has developed through focused concentration and other dedicated internal practices. People of higher soul standing have greater power to affect others for positive or negative purposes.

• **Sovereign, sovereignty** – A being who has is beholden to no higher authority, who is self-determining. One of the vulnerabilities of the human race is that we can, and have been, tricked, scared or seduced into voluntarily giving up our sovereignty. The good news is that we can take it back at any time once we are conscious of this and have clear guidance.

• **Subpersonalities** – Aspects of the human self that have its own traits, qualities and reactions. Each subpersonality can affect physiology, so that the body's state can vary when different subpersonalities are dominant.

• **TERS** – Traumatic Emotional Reintegration system developed by Greg Nevens, psychologist. An effective system using microcurrent and light therapy to rapidly clear trauma from the mind.

• **Unified field** – This refers both to theories in physics that integrate all known forces and the spiritual field of one-ness that is our true self. The unified field is larger than the physical body and includes the body. The Unified Field meditation taught in this book is a simple and effective way to be in conscious communion with the totality of your being.

• **Universal path** – Just as there is only one way to digest food even though there are countless ways to talk about food, prepare it and eat it, the universal path is the way that human beings purify their minds of blocks and limitations and awaken their consciousness to knowing who they really are. There are endless ways that people approach and talk about the universal path of course.

· **Vairagya** – Profound disillusionment that sets in after trying to find love and fulfillment outside yourself.

· **Vibrations, vibrational energy** – Oscillating energy that communicates some form of information. Vibrational energy can be very effective for healing and regenerative purposes.

· **Vipassana** – A meditation practice taught by the Buddha in which practitioners put their attention on the changing sensations in their body in a sequential manner.

· **Voluntary/involuntary functions** – Voluntary physiological functions are bodily functions we can control with our minds. Involuntary functions are those on auto-pilot that happen without any need for consciousness awareness or control.

· **Vows** – A powerful declaration made in a very focused, passionate state of mind that has ongoing binding effects on a person until it is formally revoked.

· **Witness consciousness** – An aspect of our awareness that observes all experiences of life from a place of equanimity and wisdom. A form of mindfulness.

· **Yin/Yang** – The basic polarizing force of the Universe. All material things and energetic forces are in flux between Yin and Yang. Oneness is the state of consciousness beyond duality, where Yin/Yang is no longer the reality.

· **Yogi** – A person dedicated to disciplines working with the breath, the body and consciousness.

APPENDIX 2

Resources on Your Path

BOOKS

Psychology, Traumatology

- Unlocking the Emotional Brain, Ecker, Ticic and Hulley, Routledge 2012
- The Body Keeps the Score, Bessel Van Der Kolk, Penguin Books 2014
- Energy Tapping for Trauma, Fred Gallo, New Harbinger 2007
- The Courage to Heal, Laura Davis and Ellen Bass, Harper Collins 1988
- Overcoming Trauma and PTSD, Sheela Raja, New Harbinger Press 2012
- The PTSD Workbook, Willams and Poijula, New Harbinger 2016

Vibrational Medicine

- Healing the Root of Pain, Darren Starwynn, Desert Heart Press 2013
- Microcurrent Electro-Acupuncture, Darren Starwynn, Desert Heart Press 2001
- Vibrational Medicine Richard Gerber, Bear & Company 1988

- Let There Be Light Darius Dinshah, 6th Edition, Dinshah Health Society 2001
- Golden Light Julianne Bien, Spectrahue 2004
- Light Medicine of the Future Jacob Liberman, Bear & Company 1991
- Energy Medicine, The Scientific Basis James Oschman, Churchill Livingstone 2000
- Science and Human Transformation William Tiller, Pavior 1997
- Molecules of Emotion Candace Pert, Scribner 1997
- The Process of Healing H. Van Gelder, Robert Martin Publishing 1989

Metaphysics

- The Four Agreements, Don Miguel Ruiz, Amber-Allen Publishing 1997
- The Way of Mastery, Shanti Christo Foundation 2015
- The Book of Mastery, Paul Selig, Penguin Books 2016
- The Power of Intention Wayne Dyer, Hay House 2004
- Your Soul's Plan – Discovering the Real Meaning of the Life you Planned Before you Were Born Robert Schwartz, Frog Books 2007
- The Seven Rays of Life Alice Bailey, Lucis Press 1995
- Messages From The Masters Brian Weiss, Time Warner 2000
- The Transfiguration of our World, Gordon Asher Davidson, Golden Firebird Press 2015

Scientific Papers on the Biofield, Energy Medicine and More

- See published papers by Beverly Rubik on her website: http://www.frontiersciences.org/recent-publications.html

Vipassana Meditation Training

Vipassana Meditation Retreats – 10 day silent meditation retreats are offered throughout the world by *The Art of Living*, https://www.dhamma.org. and other organizations. Vipassana cannot be adequately taught through a book and requires live training and experience. Attending a 10 day silent retreat is a very valuable, life-changing experience and I highly recommend it.

Professional Support

Professionals referred to in Section III and Foreword, and some others worth mentioning

• Greg Nevens, EDD, health psychologist, CAM Practitioner, developer of Traumatic Emotional Reintegration System (TERS). Health Psychology Center, 222 Auburn Street, Portland, ME 207.653.4301

• Darren Starwynn, O.M.D., Author, Biofield healer, vibrational medicine practitioner and spiritual counselor. Center for Health and Happiness, 131 Camino Alto, Ste G, Mill Valley, CA 94931 415.888.3891 www.drstarwynn.com Both local and remote healing and coaching sessions offered. Opt into my website as a free member to access videos and instruction sheets for the practices offered in Part II of this book, and other valuable resources.

• Susannah Redelfs, 5D Healer. Susannah was one of my teachers of 5D healing and taught me about the Unified Field meditation. She has many valuable resources on her website: http://www.councilofone.org/

• Deborah Wayne, 5D Healer. Deborah is a teacher of Biofield Healing and is the Director of the Biofield Institute. https://painfreelivingprogram.com/

• Meg Benedicte, Spiritual counselor, channel. Meg is an advanced healer who has taught me a great deal about the Light Body and spiritual activation. https://newearthcentral.com/

• Beverly Rubik, Ph.D., Holistic Health Practitioner, Educator, Scientist. Dr. Rubik offers advanced bio-energetic testing and therapies, and lifestyle recommendations. Her work includes arterial assessment, heart rate variability testing, Biofield measurements and brainwave biofeedback. www.frontiersciences.org, www.brubik.com

RECLAIMING YOUR CALM CENTER

APPENDIX 3

Words of Power

Let's revisit the book *The Four Agreements*[89] by *Ruiz* quoted earlier. The first agreement in the book is called *Be Impeccable with Your Word*. Ruiz is very clear about the power of our spoken words to bless or curse ourselves or others. If you have not read this book recently, I highly recommend it.

A vital part of reclaiming your calm center is to stop polluting it. The main way it gets polluted is by speaking and thinking negative, self-limiting messages. Thoughts are things – potent things that continually create our reality. Yes folks, it can always be spring cleaning time for our thoughts and speech.

The main expressions that pollute our calm center are:

- Gossiping
- Complaining
- Judgment
- Uninvited criticism
- Self-deprecating thoughts and comments
- Self-doubt

[89] Ruiz, Don Miguel, The Four Agreements, Amber Allen Publishing 2011

Don't feel bad if you are unable to clean up all of those right away. Self-love does not judge – it holds a space of acceptance and honoring for any effort you make. What is most important is that you intend to be impeccable with your word, as Ruiz counsels, and do your best. As your consciousness expands you will catch yourself more quickly.

Remember, many of your negative habits of thought and speaking don't even come from you. You mostly likely adopted these from people you were highly influenced by. Reclaiming your calm center includes affirming your true Self and releasing old, non-serving habits of thought and speech. Invoke your inner Witness and ask this part to alert you instantly when you are not being impeccable with your word so you can self-correct. This can be fun, like a dance you get to do all the time. Dance with your true Self, and when a negative pretender voice tries to cut in get adept at refusing him and staying with the partner you really want to be with. I once called this dance the Transformation Two-Step.

Because it is not easy to always be impeccable with our word it is very useful to regularly speak or chant words of power. These are words that rapidly bring you into alignment with the truth and spirit inside of you. These are words that empower you and affirm who you really are. Use words of power to rapidly re-align yourself when you want to affirm your good, or when if you become mindful that you are having or moving into a negative experience.

The words *"I AM"* are probably the best way to start a powerful sentence. I AM, or even using the word *"I"* is a direct connection to your true Self. Whatever you put after I AM, or I'm in a sentence has great creative power. Be careful how you use it!

It is certainly true that our ego selves can co-opt the word *"I"* and use it to limit or hurt. Be very careful about this. If appropriate it is fine to tell a trusted friend "I feel down and miserable today". Sometimes we need to share our pain with our friends and partners. Just make sure you don't start that sentence with I AM, such as "I am down and miserable today". That would be a form of cursing yourself!

According to the book of Exodus in the Bible, God used the term I AM to Moses – God said to Moses, *"I AM WHO I AM"*; and He said, *"Thus you shall say to the sons of Israel, I AM has sent me to you."* This indicates that I AM is the Divine principle within each of us. You are literally invoking the Divine when you speak words of power starting with I AM.

Words of Power

Here are some words of power that I have used and love.

- *I AM pure and perfect now and always*

- *I AM my calm center, and it feels great*

- *I AM a master being now transforming stress into joy*

- *I AM in love, I AM loved, I live in abundance always*

- *I accept my pain for value – transforming it into spiritual treasure*

- *There is nothing to heal, nothing to change, nothing to fix. I AM I AM I AM*

- *I enter into the soul of this practice easily and gracefully (as you start any of the practices in this section)*

- *Depression is the flip side of inflation. I stand in my calm center free of either polarity, in joy*

Start a notebook, or a section in your journal, for writing your favorite words of power, including affirmations. Make a commitment to read them aloud at least once a day.

- *I totally accept and believe that I can have joy in my life, and I AM perfect just the way I AM*

I suggest that you create your own words of power. Play with crafting short, powerful phrases that flow well and help you to feel uplifted when you speak them out loud.

Affirmations

Our subconscious minds hold vast creative power. Our conscious minds, that which we are aware of in our waking state, is probably about 1% as powerful as our subconscious minds. The conscious mind is like the tip of huge, hidden iceberg.

What this means is that the thoughts your conscious mind thinks have great creative power. If you keep thinking about an ideal romantic partner you would like to be with that will make you tend to attract someone like that. But if at the same time your subconscious mind is holding thoughts and pictures of you feeling unsafe with someone like that, or you being unworthy of a soul mate, that worthy partner will not come to you. The people who actually show up are more likely to be people who treat you poorly or have low self-esteem and cause more unpleasant drama in your life.

For this reason it is vital for our happiness and well-being that we deliberately infuse our subconscious minds with thoughts and images of what we DO want. Two proven ways to do that are affirmation and visualization. Affirmation is repeating phrases to yourself that infuse your subconscious mind with what you want to experience and manifest. Visualization is practicing seeing or imagining the things you want in your inner mind. The practices in this Section include many aspects of affirmation and visualization. The Words of Power above are powerful affirmations.

There are some affirmations that are more effective than others. In his book *The Success Principles*[90] Jack Canfield offers these nine guidelines for creating affirmations that will be effective for re-programming your subconscious mind. I have lightly rewritten some of his descriptions and examples to make them more in line with this book:

1. Start with the words I AM – the two most powerful words in the English language

---

[90] Canfield, Jack, The Success Principles, Harper Collins, 2005

2. Use the present tense – describe what you want as though you already have it.

Ineffective: I am now attracting my ideal soul mate

Effective: I am now with my soul mate and enjoying her company and feeling happy

3. State it in the positive - Affirm what you want, not what you don't want.

Ineffective: My pain is going away, or I AM free of pain

Effective: I enjoy and love how comfortable and pleasurable I feel in my body

Ineffective: I am no longer afraid of being in social situations

Effective: I am comfortable and at ease in any situation

4. Keep it brief - The shorter and more punchy it is, the better it will impress your subconscious mind. Think of your subconscious mind as a young child – sophisticated and esoteric phrases mean nothing to her.

5. Make it specific - Vague affirmations produce vague results.

Ineffective: I am making more money this year

Effective: I have received a raise of $35,000/year, or I Am earning over $250,000 in 2017.

6. Include an action word ending with *–ing*. Action verbs add power by evoking an image of doing it right now.

Ineffective: I express myself openly and honestly

Effective: I am confidently expressing myself openly and honestly.

7. Include at least one dynamic emotion or feeling word. - Include the emotional state you would be feeling if you had already achieved the goal.

Ineffective: I have calmed my mind and I am feeling inner peace

Effective: I am feeling luscious and joyful as I enjoy my calm center

8. Make affirmations for yourself, not others

Ineffective: My husband is being more kind and considerate to me

Effective: I am effectively communicating my needs and desires to my husband

9. Add *"or something better"* to some affirmations. What we think we want may be limited compared to what our soul wants for us. Adding these power words to the end of your affirmation leaves you open to the Universe to give you what is highest and best for you, even if you are not yet asking for it.

Ineffective: I am enjoying living in a beautiful house on a great plot of land this year in the Bay area of California.

Effective: I am enjoying living in a beautiful house on a great plot of land this year in the Bay area of California *or better.*

Decrees

Decrees are powerful statements that raise your consciousness vibration. Speaking them out loud instantly aligns you with your true Self. Here are some decrees that I have used:

• *I AM standing in my chakra pillar of light as a sovereign being NOW. I AM activating my light body and my light body is completely grounded in my physical, material reality.*

• *I AM balanced between spirit and matter, left brain and right brain and my human and divine aspects of being.*

• *I AM in my Unified Field of light always, even when I'm not consciously thinking about it.*

• *My soul is serving 24-7 and my presence brings blessings to all people and animals I come in contact with. I AM an active part of the solution on Earth now.*

• *I AM one with the forces of light that are transforming our Earth now. I AM claiming victory for light, love and redemption of the human race NOW.*

Here is an excerpt from a *"I AM"* decree offered by Patricia Cota-Robles: [91]

I AM now experiencing a higher octave of my Godhood, and my Father-Mother God are able to easily move through me. My eyes are becoming blazing Rays of Light through which the Light of God will now flow to bless all Life. My hands are becoming mighty conductors of God's Healing Power. My lips are becoming the instruments through which God's words are formed and directed into the physical plane of Earth. My feet are walking the Path of Light. My life force is NOW the vehicle through which God enters the world to Love and serve all Life.

I now realize and accept my unlimited ability to do whatever is necessary in order to establish and expand Eternal Peace and God's Infinite Abundance in my world and the worlds of all Humanity. Through my thoughts, words, actions, feelings, beliefs and memories I AM a mighty, balancing Activity of Light pulsating in, through and around every electron of Life on Earth.

Beloved I AM, Beloved I AM, Beloved I AM That I AM.

Here is another "I AM" decree that works with the transmuting spiritual power called the Violet Flame[92]:

Now in the name of Love, Wisdom, Power and Authority of the beloved, victorious presence of God I AM, I speak directly to the heart of the Violet Flame. Sacred Fire, enfold me in the purifying, forgiving, healing substance of your Light which causes the consciousness and feeling of Divine Love and Freedom to flow through me constantly to bless all life. Let this purifying

---

91 http://www.crystalwind.ca/awaken-the-soul/channeled-messages/patricia-cota-robles/co-creating-a-new-paradigm-for-2017   From Patricia Cota-Robles on www.eraofpeace.org

92 The Violet Flame is an emanation of spiritual Light that has been given to humanity in recent times. It is reputedly able to transmute all kinds of distortions in our energy fields, including old karmic residues. It is a rapid way to purify, heal and evolve. St. Germaine, a historical figure from 1700's Europe now considered to be an Ascended Master does the service of bringing the Violet Flame to humanity. Chanting I AM decrees about the Violet Flame with intent and sincerity can bring about rapid positive transformation off all the "stuff" referred to in Chapter 5.

essence saturate the atmosphere wherever I live, move, breathe and have my Being, so that its miracle-working presence will give tangible proof of your reality to all humanity.[93]

Using Words of Power

It is very hard to control the negative thoughts in our heads all the time, so a great way to keep your energy positive and vibrant is to speak words of power often. Collect those that speak to you and that work for you to bring your consciousness up.

Words of power can be used as practices you do in a meditative state. You can also start infusing your everyday communications with them. You don't need to sound pompous and preachy to do that. Simply be mindful of your words, especially how you are using "I" and "I am" in sentences. You can share powerful affirmations when you are hanging out with your friends by saying things like "I am feeling good today", "I am now creating an exciting new project" or "I am excited about going to the movie with you tonight."

One of the most common questions in our society is "How are you?" or "How's it going?". Most of the time we answer with semi-truthful, reflexive answers like "fine", "not too bad" or programmed negative ones like "ahh, life's tough all over". Why not use those times when people ask you how you are to speak some words of power? The next time someone says to you "how are you" you could say something like "Excellent – I AM happy to be alive and enjoying my calm center." Now, that could be a good conversation starter!

---

[93] This decree was given to me by DaVid Rafael, director of The Light Party. There are many valuable resources on his website: http://www.lightparty.com/

Deprogramming Negative Beliefs

This is a simple, valuable sequence of three statements you can use anytime to de-program negative beliefs you become aware of having. Make these three statements, and fill in the blanks as instructed. Continue making these statements for addressing related aspects of the negative belief, or other beliefs, until you feel complete.

Statement 1: It is my intention, as the Master Being that I AM, to release my beliefs in the reasons why I am _____ *(fill in negative belief or experience)*

Statement 2: I now totally accept and believe that _____ *(flip negative belief/experience into a positive affirmation)*

Statement 3: I now totally accept and believe that I can have joy in my life, and that I am perfect just the way I am

Example for person stressing about finances:

It is my intention, as the Master Being that I AM, to release my beliefs in the reasons why I am poor and struggling for money.
I now totally accept and believe that I am connected with infinite resourcefulness, and that all I need to know to thrive is before me now
I now totally accept and believe that I can have joy in my life, and that I am perfect just the way I am

Example for person feeling rejected by a lover:

It is my intention, as the Master Being that I AM, to release my beliefs in the reasons why I am rejected and unworthy of being loved for who I am

I now totally accept and believe that I am a beautiful, loving and worthy person who is loved by God and those close to me just for being me.

I now totally accept and believe that I can have joy in my life, and that I am perfect just the way I am

Manifestation Command

Manifest, manifest, manifest! Physically, tangibly, materially, financially, lovingly before me in my life:

The abundance, the growth, the connectedness and the prosperity that I seek, with grace and with ease, immediately before me – So It Is!

Command to Clear Your Energy Field

I command, in the name of the Divine (or substitute any other power you wish to invoke such as God, Christ, Archangel Michael, etc.,) that any negative energies, cords, webs, sticky residues or any other influences not of the Light, coming from (put name or names if you know where these energies have come from, leave out if you don't know), be completely removed from my physical, mental, emotional and spiritual bodies NOW, purified through the Violet Flame (or other purifying spiritual power) and returned to Source transformed by Unconditional Love. I request and command the White Light of God to surround and protect me.

Notes

1. This command can help you or a client take charge of their own energy field and use their inner soul power to clear themselves. In cases where the negative energy is of a higher level than you or

they can deal with, it is important to get help from someone of a high enough soul standing to be able to help you safely clear. It is possible to use kinesiology or other form of dowsing to ask if it is appropriate for you or the client to clear the negative energy themselves, or if higher level help is needed.

2. If you are a doctor or holistic health professionals I DO NOT recommend that you attempt to clear for your clients unless you have very specialized training and empowerment in this area. Doing so could be dangerous to your own well-being. It is far safer to guide the client in doing it for themselves.

3. The safest and one of the most important ways to clear negative energies is Forgiveness Practice, described in *Chapter 13*. Even when the above command is used, or a high level helper is called up, forgiveness should still be practiced to help heal on the soul level.

About Darren Starwynn

Darren Starwynn is the author of three books and inventor of several innovative energy medical devices used worldwide. He is a graduate of American School of Oriental Medicine, Tri-State Institute of Traditional Chinese Medicine and received his certification as Oriental Medical Doctor (O.M.D.) at the National Academy for Advanced Asian Medicine. Darren has over 30 years experience in the fields of acupuncture, vibrational medicine and spiritual healing. He has led hundreds of educational workshops for physicians and the public.

A lifelong meditator, Darren is dedicated to helping his clients release old trauma, pain and limitations while supporting them in discovering and fulfilling their most inspired life purpose. His greatest passion is helping others awaken the true Self they really are. He maintains a private practice in Mill Valley, California and also offers remote healing sessions throughout the world.

Darren loves hiking in the mountains, playing guitar, drumming, bringing people together in spiritual community and helping them laugh their way to illumination.

Other Books by Darren Starwynn

1. *Healing the Root of Pain*, Darren Starwynn, Desert Heart Press 2013

This is a how-to book written for holistic health professionals and psychologists wishing to learn a highly effective new method to support the healing of trauma and emotional imbalances using vibrational medicine. It is also suitable for people wishing to heal themselves.

2. Microcurrent Electro-Acupuncture, Darren Starwynn, Desert Heart Press 2001
A pioneering manual for acupuncturists and holistic health professionals providing theory, research and detailed instructions in performing a new system of non-needle acupuncture using microcurrent therapies.

About Beverly Rubik

Dr. Beverly Rubik earned her Ph.D. in biophysics in 1979 at the University of California at Berkeley. She has published over 100 scientific papers and 2 books. She is president and founder of the Institute for Frontier Science, a 501c3 nonprofit research laboratory in Emeryville, California.

She serves on the editorial boards of several integrative medicine journals and the Journal of Vortex Science and Technology. She is a professor at Energy Medicine University in Sausalito, CA. Dr. Rubik is also an adjunct faculty member serving doctoral students in the College of Integrative Medicine and Health Sciences at Saybrook University in Oakland, CA. Her main focus is on subtle energies and energy medicine and the possible hazardous effects of electromagnetic pollution. She also conducts research on maverick health care products and maintains a small holistic health practice.

Websites
www.frontiersciences.org
www.brubik.com

INDEX

Made in the USA
Middletown, DE
21 September 2022

10906500R00166